Extension Ministers
Mr. Wesley's True Heirs

Extension Ministers
Mr. Wesley's True Heirs

RUSSELL E. RICHEY

General Board of Higher Education and Ministry
The United Methodist Church
Nashville, Tennessee

The General Board of Higher Education and Ministry leads and serves The United Methodist Church in the recruitment, preparation, nurture, education, and support of Christian leaders—lay and clergy—for the work of making disciples of Jesus Christ for the transformation of the world. Its vision is that a new generation of Christian leaders will commit boldly to Jesus Christ and be characterized by intellectual excellence, moral integrity, spiritual courage, and holiness of heart and life.

The General Board of Higher Education and Ministry of The United Methodist Church is the church's agency for educational, institutional, and ministerial leadership. It serves as an advocate for the intellectual life of the church. The Board's mission embodies the Wesleyan tradition of commitment to the education of laypersons and ordained persons by providing access to higher education for all persons.

This book expands the essay "Are Extension Ministries an Opportunity to Reclaim a Wesleyan Understanding of Mission?" by Russell E. Richey, in *Questions for the Twenty-First Century Church*, eds. Russell E. Richey, William B. Lawrence, and Dennis M. Campbell (Nashville: Abingdon Press, 1999). Used by permission from Abingdon Press.

All scripture quotations unless noted otherwise are taken from the *New Revised Standard Version of the Bible*, copyright 1989, Division of Christian Education of the National Council of the Churches of Christ in the United States of America. Used by permission. All rights reserved.

ISBN: 978-0-938162-88-9

Produced by the Office of Interpretation
Manufactured in the United States of America

Contents

Abbreviations

For Denominations

AME	The African Methodist Episcopal Church (1816–)
AMEZ	The African Methodist Episcopal Church Zion (1820–)
CME	The (Colored) Christian Methodist Episcopal Church (1870–)
EA	The Evangelical Association/Church (1803–1946)
EUBC	The Evangelical United Brethren Church (1946–1968)
MC	The Methodist Church, USA (1939–1968)
MEC	The Methodist Episcopal Church (1784–1939)
MECS	The Methodist Episcopal Church, South (1844–1939)
MPC	The Methodist Protestant Church (1830–1939)
UBC	The United Brethren Church (1800–1946)
UMC	The United Methodist Church (1968–)

For Denominational Periodicals and Journals

CA *Christian Advocate,* New York (MEC)

MQR Refers to the quarterly theological journal of the MEC under its fluctuating names (*Methodist Magazine, Methodist Review, Methodist Quarterly Review*)

For Other Publications

Bangs, *History* Nathan Bangs, *A History of the Methodist Episcopal Church*, 12th ed., 4 vols. (New York: Carlton & Porter, 1860).

Discipline/ church year Book of Discipline (under slightly varying names) for the denomination cited; e.g., *Discipline*/UMC 1996.

EWM	Nolan B. Harmon et al., *The Encyclopedia of World Methodism*, 2 vols. Sponsored by the World Methodist Council and the Commission on Archives and History, UMC (Nashville: The United Methodist Publishing House, 1974).
JGC/Church year	Refers to the *Journal of the General Conference of The Methodist Episcopal Church* for the church and year indicated. Includes citations from *Journals of the General Conference of the Methodist Episcopal Church, 1796–1856*, 3 vols. (New York: Carlton & Phillips, 1856). Vol. 1, 1796–1836; Vol. 2, 1840–1844; Vol. 3, 1848–1856.
JLFA	*The Journal and Letters of Francis Asbury*, ed. Elmer T. Clark, 3 vols. (London: Epworth; and Nashville: Abingdon, 1958).
Minutes/ church/year	Annual or General Minutes however titled and aggregated. Reference for the early years of the MEC is to *Minutes of the Annual Conferences of the Methodist Episcopal Church for the Years 1773–1828* (New York: T. Mason and G. Lane, 1840) unless alternative edition indicated. For example, reference for 1784 in *Minutes of the Methodist Conferences, Annually Held in America; From 1773 to 1813, Inclusive* (New York: Published by Daniel Hitt & Thomas Ware for the Methodist Connexion in The United States, 1813) as *Minutes*/MEC/1784 (1813).

Introduction

Mr. Wesley's True Heirs: Extension Ministers

Luke 9:1-6

[1]Then Jesus called the twelve together and gave them power and authority over all demons and to cure diseases, [2]and he sent them out to proclaim the kingdom of God and to heal. [3]He said to them, "Take nothing for your journey, no staff, nor bag, nor bread, nor money—not even an extra tunic. [4]Whatever house you enter, stay there, and leave from there. [5]Wherever they do not welcome you, as you are leaving that town shake the dust off your feet as a testimony against them." [6]They departed and went through the villages, bringing the good news and curing diseases everywhere.

Luke 10:1-12

[1]After this the Lord appointed seventy others and sent them on ahead of him in pairs to every town and place where he himself intended to go. [2]He said to them, "The harvest is plentiful, but the laborers are few; therefore ask the Lord of the harvest to send out laborers into his harvest. [3]Go on your way. See, I am sending you out like lambs into the midst of wolves. [4]Carry no purse, no bag, no sandals; and greet no one on the road. [5]Whatever house you enter, first say, 'Peace to this house!' [6]And if anyone is there who shares in peace, your peace will rest on that person; but if not, it will return to you. [7]Remain in the same house, eating and drinking whatever they provide, for the laborer deserves to be paid. Do not move about from house to house. [8]Whenever you enter a town and its people welcome you, eat what is set before you; [9]cure the sick who are there, and say to them, 'The kingdom of God has come near to you.' [10]But whenever you enter a

town and they do not welcome you, go out into its streets and say, [11]"Even the dust of your town that clings to our feet, we wipe off in protest against you. Yet know this: the kingdom of God has come near." [12]I tell you, on that day it will be more tolerable for Sodom than for that town."

—⚬—

1 JESUS, Thy wandering sheep behold![1]
    See, Lord, with tenderest pity see
The sheep that cannot find the fold,
    Till sought and gathered in by Thee.

2 Lost are they now, and scattered wide,
    In pain, and weariness, and want;
With no kind shepherd near to guide
    The sick, and spiritless, and faint.

3 Thou, only Thou, the kind and good
    And sheep-redeeming Shepherd art:
Collect Thy flock, and give them food,
    And pastors after Thine own heart.

4 Give the pure word of general grace,
    And great shall be the preachers' crowd;
Preachers, who all the sinful race
    Point to the all-atoning blood.

5 Open their mouth, and utterance give;
    Give them a trumpet-voice, to call
On all mankind to turn and live,
    Through faith in Him who died for all.

6 Thy only glory let them seek;
    O let their hearts with love o'erflow!
Let them believe, and therefore speak,
    And spread Thy mercy's praise below.[2]

This little book concerns the ministry of The United Methodist Church within the United States and particularly that exercised by a significant cohort of the elders, or presbyters: those who function primarily as military or college or hospital chaplains; teachers, deans, or presidents; staff in denominational agencies; heads of camps, homes, or nursing facilities; social workers—the list goes on. Such vocations the 2004 *Book of Discipline of The United Methodist Church* defines as "extension ministries." It includes within this category quite a range of vocations and offices, including district superintendents and other key members of a bishop's cabinet or extended cabinet. And it now distinguishes appointments within the connectional structures from those serving beyond the connectional system—those under endorsement by the General Board of Higher Education and Ministry (as above), those under the General Board of Global Ministries, and those beyond such close affiliations but yet considered by bishop and board of ordained ministry "to be a true extension of the Christian ministry of the Church" (¶344).

Extension ministers, ordained as elders and in full connection, share with United Methodist elders generally the long-used Methodist twofold ministerial authorization—presbyteral ordination and membership in an annual conference. Extension ministers differ from their annual conference colleagues, however (and typically), in manner of appointment, primary accountability, and salary source. The "regular," non-extension elder typically

- is appointed by a bishop at annual conference and is sent (or itinerates) to a congregational or other setting in missionary fashion;
- is salaried by that institution;
- is held accountable by its pastor- or staff-parish relations committee;
- is overseen by the bishop and district superintendent;
- reports to and is subject to discipline by the annual conference; and
- remains as an itinerant minister and potentially at least available for reappointment to another setting at the following conference.

Appointment and itinerancy[3] make ministry in the Wesleyan and Methodist communions quite different from the more typical "call" pattern in

American Protestantism. Sent out from annual conference, not called by a congregation, Methodist ministers can appropriately be termed missionaries.

Theoretically, appointment and itinerancy apply in some sense to the extension categories mentioned above, as the following statement from United Methodism's *Book of Discipline* makes clear:

Section X. Appointments to Extension Ministries

¶343. *Appointments Extending the Ministry of The United Methodist Church*—1. Elders in effective relationship may be appointed to serve in ministry settings beyond the local United Methodist church in the witness and service of Christ's love and justice. Persons in these appointments remain within the itineracy and shall be accountable to the annual conference. They shall be given the same moral and spiritual support by it as are persons in appointments to pastoral charges. Their effectiveness shall be evaluated in the context of the specific setting in which their ministry is performed.[4]

Notwithstanding this "conference" embrace, the extension ministers (many of them anyway, for instance, chaplains)

- are hired, salaried, and supervised by their employing institution;
- enjoy multiyear or open contracts;
- receive credentialing from and remain accountable to a certifying authority that serves that profession;
- place their primary identity in and regularly associate with others in that profession; and
- may wear garb or enjoy perks peculiar to that role.

Do extension ministers really belong within the United Methodist clergy fold and the Wesleyan understanding of itinerancy? If so, how? Have extension ministries always been so clearly differentiated from the other clergy? When and how did they emerge? And were they then so marginalized? Are they afterthoughts in the Methodist ministerial scheme? How have we come to the current situation?

Why, furthermore, do persons serving in such roles not rather enjoy the status and belong within the order of ordained deacons, whom the church sets apart for a lifetime of servant leadership and ministries of Word and Service? (*Discipline*/UMC 2004, ¶¶328, 329).

> Deacons fulfill servant ministry in the world and lead the Church in relating the gathered life of Christians to their ministries in the world, interrelating worship in the gathered community with service to God in the world. (*Discipline*/UMC 2004, ¶328)

Do not the aforementioned extension ministries fit into the following two "primary fields" of service into which deacons in full connection may be appointed?

> *a)* Through agencies and settings beyond the local church that extend the witness and service of Christ's love and justice in the world by equipping all Christians to fulfill their own calls to Christian service; or
>
> *b)* Through United Methodist Church-related agencies, schools, colleges, theological schools, ecumenical agencies . . . (*Discipline*/UMC 2004, ¶331)

And do not the typical extension ministries accord with deacons' non-itinerant status, professional style, and responsibilities for participating in their own placement? Why do we have extension ministries within the elders' order at all?

We will return to some of these questions in the final chapter, particularly those concerning which vocations for extension ministries belong within the elders' and which within the deacons' orders. However, while the issue of the relation of the two orders will come up briefly in several places, this book will not really treat the new office of permanent deacon. Rather, it focuses on the factors that have led to the present confusion and treats the prior history when, with a transitional diaconate and no real option for full connection other than through the elder's order, the church generated extension ministry after extension ministry. One might pose interesting counterfactual questions and ask what the landscape of ministry would look like today had Methodism possessed a permanent deacon's order from the start, had it had a non-itinerating ministerial status within which to accommodate needed specializations, and had it been able to create vocations that extended the church's witness into the world within the diaconate. A larger book than this could take on such queries and map the entire landscape of Methodist and United Methodist ministry, from old and new lay offices through to the district superintendency and episcopacy. In this more modest enterprise, I will focus on extension ministry in relation to the elder, or presbyter.[5]

THE PUZZLE

In the following pages, we will explore an irony, a puzzle, a concern: roles and offices that American Methodism created to function connectionally, that emerged because the "connection"—the church as a whole—needed them, that held things together, that occupied the center, that gave the church leadership have in the late twentieth and early twenty-first centuries become peripheral.

As we shall see, historically, Methodism in North America established extension ministries to serve the connection. Into these highly salient offices it put its ministerial talent. From these roles it expected and received connectional leadership. Today the church struggles to determine their place. The recent designating categories illustrate the uncertainty: *special appointments, appointments beyond the local church, extension ministries.* A joke or gibe conveys the commonly held perception. Sometimes it is posed as a question, sometimes said with sadness, sometimes with a little bite to it, sometimes really for humor: "Do I understand correctly that you will be moving into chaplaincy (taking a position at the seminary, going with a Nashville board, becoming a nursing facility administrator . . .)? You have so much promise. I hate to see you leave the ministry."

Such attitudes prevail because extension ministries have evolved; and, in some few instances, evolved in directions that justify legitimate concern from those who care deeply about our connection. In the rare case, a person retaining ordination as an elder continues to claim the status, conference relation, and tax preference, but has "evolved" away from meaningful connection to United Methodism, much less to real exercise of the duties expected of the presbyter. The ministry exercised by these few, if such it really is, may look like that to which all Christians are called and, to that extent, scarcely warrants ordination and conference membership. Thankfully the new Disciplinary categorizations and greater vigilance on the part of boards of ordained ministry root out the few such bad apples.

Unfortunately, anecdotes about "straying" elders, the necessity of policing conference membership, and the presumption that real ministry is parish ministry have led some boards of ordained ministry and district committees on ministry to resist accepting persons for candidacy who profess interest in vocations that fit within extension ministry—or to resist accepting them unless they commit to serving a local church first or unless they will select the deacon's track. The latter resistance, we should note, is understandable as the ministry of extension elders, in some circumstances, does look like that of the permanent deacon. And the *Discipline*'s treatment of the office and work of the ordained deacon in ¶¶328 and 331 lends itself to confusion. Particularly unhelpful is the use of the problematic language of "beyond the local church" in ¶331, terminology that effectively makes parish ministry normative also for the deacon. The parish norm and delineation of roles similar to that of elder have apparently led some congregations and clergy to employ deacons in positions that would seemingly call for elders. Uncertainties expressed by boards of ordained ministries about the whether and where of extension ministry are therefore understandable, as are their concerns about the distant relation of many extension ministers to the conference. Indeed, comparing extension ministers to deacons highlights the marginal character of the former. By contrast, those in the relatively new order of deacon, now with their own ordination and full conference membership, live with higher expectations about accountability, reporting, and connection (to the conference, to the board of ordained ministry, and to the Order of Deacons) than do extension ministers.

Moreover, the connectionally minded, and especially bishops and cabinets, cannot help being concerned by the sheer number of those in the several extension categories (currently 3,314) for whom appointments would now be required should they so request. Of that total, 464 serve as district superintendents, but almost four times that number (1,595) belong to the "other extension ministry" category. Just under 20 percent of the total cohort of active elders (17,098) function in extension ministries.[6] Little real danger lurks in the possibility that the amassed numbers of special or extension ministers would collectively seek appointments, but the possibility remains—a thinkable worry. More to the point, the numbers and percentage should indicate that the role and category should not be ignored.

The problems in fitting extension ministers into the conference order have as much to do with the behavior of those of us "specials" as with boards of ordained ministry and bishops. At least in my own experience, those of us in extension ministries now find it difficult to figure out how we "connect" and how we might play constructive roles on local, district, and conference levels, particularly the latter two. We perform our ministries faithfully. We report to the board of ordained ministry and the district superintendent on forms and in categories focused on the local church and largely unexpressive of our ministerial functions. We attend the annual conference breakfast or luncheon. We listen attentively to speeches affirming the importance of our offices and claiming our connection. We depart the sacrament of our inclusion full of the conference's food, reminded that we are indeed set apart—far apart—from "real" ministry, emptied again of any sense of really belonging, and implicitly, at least, given leave to leave. Conference won't miss us.

We will attend in later chapters to the evolution and gradual expansion of extension ministries and the stretching of the connectional bonds. The yawning distance between regular and special appointments has to do with changes that have happened to all ministries—to those exercising responsibilities in the local church as well as to those in extension roles. The attitudes conveyed by the joke mentioned above implicitly reveal a great deal about the speaker, conveying just how much itinerancy and regular appointments have changed. A great reversal has occurred, as we shall see. Now "traveling" preachers have effectively "located" to the parish. "Itinerants" travel within and for the local church. The transformations in Methodist, now United Methodist, ministry to which we will of necessity attend below have virtually returned itinerancy to the parish style of Mr. Wesley's Anglicanism. In using the earlier designation "appointments beyond the local church" (often abbreviated ABLC), United Methodism owned up with a sort of sad, unreflective candor to its narrow and limited definition of ministry, that is, ministry trimmed to parish ministry. The happier and theologically more expressive Disciplinary rubric "extension ministries" has yet to reshape attitudes and practice. And though potentially expressive, it remains defined over and against "regular" appointments.

"Special," "ABLC," "extension" ministry (call it what you will)—those of us who occupy such roles remain categorized by gibe more than by doctrine. We are defined negatively, lumped together. To our annual extension ministries breakfast come persons whom I will not see again until the same occasion next year. Military chaplains, campus ministers, teachers, administrators of our institutions, hospital chaplains, connectional officers—we share virtually nothing in common except that we retain our appointments beyond the local church. Or, more properly, our discrete identities constitute a professional grouping with its own entry procedures, professional meetings, duties and responsibilities, practices and skill sets, connectional networks, publications, and ethical expectations.

THE FIRST EXTENSION MINISTER: JOHN WESLEY

By contrast, if one focuses explicitly on Mr. Wesley himself, one could well argue, as indeed I will here, that those of us in extension ministries remain the true heirs to John Wesley. Who more than he ministered "beyond the local church"? We carry on his extension work as teacher, publisher, missionary, fundraiser, administrator of the connection, and chaplain for the people called Methodist. The chapters that follow will then attempt a variety of things. We will explore the Wesley-like duties for which the church found that it needed persons full time. Into these foundational and connectional offices the church put its talent, often encouraging and expecting multiple leadership roles, not simply the single authorized function.

There were ambiguities or uncertainties in connectional appointments from the start. I will show from the record that the church struggled with how best to oversee and keep accountable those charged with tasks that lay beyond the normal circuit assignments. Methodism made some offices elective by General Conference. Others that functioned on a regional or conference level remained under the bishops and by appointment. The church housed these "special" appointments in close connection with "fellow" itinerants whose proximity permitted them to provide counsel and oversight. In addition, those persons in these connectional roles remained accountable to their annual conferences. So the special appointments connected personally, locally, on a conference level, and to the general church. They were preeminently connectional, and multidimensionally so.

I'll demonstrate that such multidimensionality gradually eroded, though even to the present the rare virtuoso individual in extension ministry will shine in an assigned role, in the local church, on district and conference levels, and for the general church as well. Such virtuosity notwithstanding, various forces complicated and frustrated the church's efforts to stay connected with those in special roles and their efforts to exercise connectional leadership. The trends that remade special ministry and marginalized it are those that reshaped the church:

- centralization and bureaucratization under the General Conference
- professionalization of ministries and realignment of loyalties into professional networks
- addition of laity to what had been a ministerial guild (conference)
- jurisdictionalizing of staffing
- growth of conferences
- increasing number of special ministries and of persons in special ministries
- growing focus on the local church
- growth of some local churches into large, highly complex, multi-staffed corporations

Recent additions to the catalog of front-burner factors with which the church must contend and that push extension ministry back on the stove are the permanent deacon and its best uses, the growing number of local pastors, the church's continuing difficulties in its effective utilization and promotion of women ministers, and contests over gays and lesbians in ministry. In adjudicating intra-ministry turf wars, emotion-tinged "rights" language gets pushed to the fore—sacramental rights, voting rights, rights in the appointment process, rights to be ordained. Concerns about extension ministries rarely surface, or occasionally get tracked into one of these tense contests. For instance, in the give-and-take of the debate about who should pursue the deacon track, some suggest that those now entertaining extension ministry should invariably "go deacon." And for good or ill, extension ministry becomes a rubric under which individuals whom the church has trouble placing or who experience regular appointments at difficult places find freedom to experiment with new styles of ministry.

Underlying the argument of this book are several convictions about our connection and our connectionalism. The first, one that I have voiced in various contexts and in several essays, is that vital connectionalism remains a key factor in the overall health and well-being of Methodism. Indeed, as practiced ecclesiology, connectionalism sustains United Methodist belief in and understanding of itself, its mission, its vision, and its hope.[7] Increasingly, connectionalism is being eroded by the trajectories of both local church and extension ministries. United Methodists have as much to lose, I suggest, from excessive localism as from ministries that no longer can or do honor their originating connectional purposes. But like ministry, connectionalism has not been static over time. Different "connecting" instrumentalities emerged to give life to the church's witness, several of these instrumentalities now defined as extension ministry. Change therefore can come. And change in one part of our connection and connectionalism tends to affect the whole.

A second conviction, and concession, is that those of us in such special or ABLC or extension ministries at points have been derelict in exercising responsibility for defining and enhancing our place within Methodist connectionalism. We—or, perhaps I should say I—have sometimes been prone to play our professorial roles and leave them there and have not been very eager to exercise connectional roles. Ought we in extension roles to be helping the church envision how our special assignments serve the connection as a whole? I think so. This little book will, then, "exhort" (to use a good Methodist term) us "specials" to explore our connectional responsibilities as well as to urge for greater acceptance of our connectional roles.

AFTERWORD

I intend the appeal to Wesley in title and argument not to upset or anger my colleagues in ministry but to begin a process of posing some questions about extension ministry. I undertake this rethinking to encourage the reintegration of extension ministries into our connectional system. And I intend to encourage those of us whom the church has blessed with this special standing to take some real responsibility in helping the connection rethink how and where we belong. To that end, in order to ground our thinking, the introduction and each chapter begin with a selection from Scripture and a Charles Wesley hymn. So I undertake this little book as an experiment in quadrilateral thinking, invoking Scripture, appealing to our Wesleyan tradition, drawing on our corporate experience, and reasoning with the insights thereby garnered. The Quadrilateral, if indeed it should be our hermeneutic, requires us to be explicit in our appeal to and use of Scripture, Tradition, Experience, and Reason.

To that end this introduction begins with Jesus sending the Twelve and then the seventy into the world to preach and to heal. The passage has rich resonances with Methodism's understandings of itinerancy, evangelism, and mission. It also "extends" ministry into the healing roles so characteristic of today's chaplaincies. Similarly, Charles Wesley's hymn calls us into the ministry of the great Shepherd to reach the lost, the sick, the spiritless, the faint. The ministries within the fold and beyond the fold belong together. The pastor needs the chaplain, and the chaplain the pastor. In a later chapter I return to more extended examination of the Quadrilateral and of thinking quadrilaterally about extension ministry.

1

Connectional Tasks and Accountability

Acts 11:1-18

[1]Now the apostles and the believers who were in Judea heard that the Gentiles had also accepted the word of God. [2]So when Peter went up to Jerusalem, the circumcised believers criticized him, [3]saying, "Why did you go to uncircumcised men and eat with them?" [4]Then Peter began to explain it to them, step by step, saying, [5]"I was in the city of Joppa praying, and in a trance I saw a vision. There was something like a large sheet coming down from heaven, being lowered by its four corners; and it came close to me. [6]As I looked at it closely I saw four-footed animals, beasts of prey, reptiles, and birds of the air. [7]I also heard a voice saying to me, 'Get up, Peter; kill and eat.' [8]But I replied, 'By no means, Lord; for nothing profane or unclean has ever entered my mouth.' [9]But a second time the voice answered from heaven, 'What God has made clean, you must not call profane.' [10]This happened three times; then everything was pulled up again to heaven. [11]At that very moment three men, sent to me from Caesarea, arrived at the house where we were. [12]The Spirit told me to go with them and not to make a distinction between them and us. These six brothers also accompanied me, and we entered the man's house. [13]He told us how he had seen the angel standing in his house and saying, 'Send to Joppa and bring Simon, who is called Peter; [14]he will give you a message by which you and your entire household will be saved.' [15]And as I began to speak, the Holy Spirit fell upon them just as it had upon us at the beginning. [16]And I remembered the word of the Lord, how he had said, 'John baptized with water, but you will be baptized with the Holy Spirit.' [17]If then God gave them the same gift that he gave us

when we believed in the Lord Jesus Christ, who was I that I could hinder God?" [18]When they heard this, they were silenced. And they praised God, saying, "Then God has given even to the Gentiles the repentance that leads to life."

—∞—

1 Father, Son, and Spirit, hear[1]
   Faith's effectual fervent prayer!
   Hear, and our petitions seal;
   Let us now the answer feel.

2 Still our fellowship increase,
   Knit us in the bond of peace,
   Join our new-born spirits, join
   Each to each, and all to thine!

3 Build us in one body up,
   Called in one high calling's hope:
   One the Spirit whom we claim,
   One the pure baptismal flame;

4 One the faith and common Lord,
   One the Father lives adored,
   Over, through, and in us all,
   God incomprehensible.

5 One with God, the source of bliss,
   Ground of our communion this;
   Life of all that live below,
   Let thine emanations flow!

6 Rise eternal in our heart!
   Thou our long sought Eden art:
   Father, Son, and Holy Ghost,
   Be to us what Adam lost!

Very early, the American Methodist movement came to some important recognitions: (1) To function effectively it had to undertake some duties, tasks, and roles of a connectional nature in service to the entire connection. (2) Some of these connectional duties needed full-time staffing and tenure of more than one year. (3) The exercise of such responsibilities belonged to or was appropriately undertaken by ministers; that is, by those who enjoyed the status of membership in an annual conference and of a traveling preacher. (4) Persons under such appointment had to be made accountable to the connection in some fashion.

The accountability in one such post—one coeval with the new Methodist Episcopal Church (MEC)—was straightforward. A preacher was given a connectional position to travel with bishops Francis Asbury, Thomas Coke, or Richard Whatcoat, among them Harry Hosier, Jesse Lee, and Nicholas Snethen. Accountability—daily, indeed hourly—was built into that assignment. But what about a person to superintend the book business (publishing house)? What about preachers sent beyond conference limits as missionaries? What about assignments that did not travel with the bishops? Who or what would oversee such connectional work?

What was unclear then, and has remained unclear to this day, is how best substantively and structurally to care for that connectional accountability. How were and how are those of us in "special" appointments to exercise these responsibilities in truly connectional fashion? How should they and we be connected and where should we report—on the most general (connectional) level, primarily to the annual conference, or most directly to local Methodism? And to whom or what—bishops, presiding elders (now district superintendents), other ministers, a committee, a board, a conference?

SPECIAL APPOINTMENTS: WESLEY'S ROLES

That American Methodism would struggle to find ways of structuring these connectional roles should not surprise us. After all, the roles had inhered in an office that American Methodism never fully replicated, namely, that of John Wesley. Wesley personified the connection and exercised its key supportive roles. He served as the movement's publisher, expanding from the printing of his own writing and his brother's hymns into a range of materials for both preachers and laypeople and establishing printed works as the criteria for Methodist orthodoxy. He directed the mission of the movement and was its chief missionary. He served as its primary fund-raiser—elaborating the class from a money-raising meeting to pay for the New Room, finding ways to support other chapels and the school, and seeking resources to care for those in need. He directed the organizational life of Methodism. He constituted the faculty for the preachers, though delegating that role for lower schools to others. He was chaplain through correspondence as well as in person.

These were the roles over the course of the nineteenth century to which American Methodists gave "special" status:

> publisher,
> missionaries
> fund-raisers (colporteurs) for colleges and secondary schools,
> corresponding (general) secretaries of Methodist and interdenominational
> missionary, Bible, tract, and Sunday-School societies
> faculty in Methodist schools
> chaplains (prison or army).[2]

To be sure, both Thomas Coke and Francis Asbury aspired to Wesley's mantle and in various ways sought to superintend in a Wesleyan fashion. They—or, at least, Asbury—succeeded in the superintending role, effectively sustaining through the safeguarded appointive power the role as chief missionary and oversight of Methodism's intrinsic missionary style. A variety of factors, however, frustrated their/his efforts to carry on the variety of roles that Wesley had exercised, with publishing presenting the first and the key challenge. Travel (Asbury on the move across the expanding American movement, Coke frequently across the Atlantic) made ongoing direction quite impossible and required them to communicate on publishing concerns and other connectional matters by correspondence—a very slow process. Coke, with his Oxford education in law and divinity, had the ability to function in Wesley's stead had American Methodists been willing to permit it or had he invested sufficiently in the American movement to earn that trust. Neither occurred. Asbury, educated in the saddle like his American colleagues, gave what attention he could to publishing (as his correspondence will show), but quickly discovered that the task needed to be delegated. Furthermore, the American conferences—empowered by the precedent of 1784, by the assumed power to legislate through conferences, and eventually by the *Discipline* and the Restrictive Rules—claimed their own role in determining what Methodism would print and Methodists would read.

THE EMERGENCE OF CONNECTIONAL, OR "EXTENSION," APPOINTMENTS

The *Minutes* for The Methodist Episcopal Church (MEC) for 1789, in answer to the standard query "Where are the Preachers stationed this year?" buried in the list of appointments the notation, "Philip Cox, Book-Steward." For 1790 it listed separately and under three districts Philip Cox and William Thomas as "Travelling Book-Steward" and "John Dickins, Superintendent of the Printing and Book-business." So the *Minutes* buried the assignments, as they did again in 1791, simply listing Dickins, the book steward or agent, in Philadelphia, but grouped with others under the presiding elder of that district. (For the connectional nature of Dickins's work, see the appendix at the end of this chapter.) Over the next several years, Dickins and associates in the book effort were so identified but listed last or first in the district so as to distinguish them as "special." In 1797, in addition to the book stewards, who were listed as previously at the end of one of the districts, the *Minutes* also noted for one of the Virginia districts: "Jesse Lee is recommended by the yearly conference to travel with Bishop Asbury this year." The *Minutes* for that year also carried a special paragraph about the book operation in Philadelphia, as we will note in a moment.

In 1798, the *Minutes* answered the customary query "Where are the Preachers stationed this year?" with an interesting and important declaration up front, immediately after the question—that is, at the head of all connectional appointments: "Jesse Lee travels with Bishop Asbury." The next year, to the standard query "Where are the Preachers stationed this year?" the *Minutes* again put first and prominently:

> Jesse Lee travels with Bishop Asbury.
> Ezekiel Cooper, Editor and General Book Steward.

In 1800, the note up front identified the three bishops—Richard Whatcoat, along with Coke and Asbury. However, again for 1801 the answer was

> Thomas Coke, by consent of the general conference is in Europe.
> Nicholas Snethen travels with Bishop Asbury.
> S. Hutchinson travels with Bishop Whatcoat.
> Ezekiel Cooper superintends the printing and book business.[3]

Neither the provision for a traveling companion for the bishops nor the arrangement for a book steward was new.[4] What *was* new was the organizational or conceptual treatment of the special appointment for Ezekiel Cooper. In making provision for what we now term "extension ministries" or "appointments beyond the local church," the *Minutes* visualized Cooper's appointment and those of the bishops' aides as not just "within the connectional structures" but specifically in relation to the connection as a whole. The *Minutes* isolated Cooper, as book agent, along with the episcopal companions, as in service of the connection, though continuing in the traveling relation and serving under appointment. These two *Minutes*, then, 1799 and 1801, trumpeted the connectional nature of the duties by lodging that assignment first, right after the question and before the long list of other appointments.

The next year, in 1802, the *Minutes* buried that connectional assignment in the list of appointments, listing it as one of the assignments on the Philadelphia District: "Ezekiel Cooper, superintendent of the Printing and Book-Concern."[5] The following year the *Minutes* struggled with another special assignment that it nevertheless located within the conference listings. That year four persons carried the designation "missionary" after their names: Shadrach Bostwick on the Deerfield circuit of the Pittsburgh District, and Samuel Merwin, Elijah Chichester, and Laban Clark on the Montreal, St. John's, and Soreille circuits of the Pittsfield District.[6]

There were good reasons, as we note below, for recognizing the local basis and located base of the connectional assignments that did not constantly and physically travel. So, in 1804, the church again accented the relation of book agents to presiding elder and district. That year the *Minutes* recorded Ezekiel Cooper and John Wilson as editor and general book-steward and assistant, respectively, and listed them in New York, along with three others assigned there as preachers—N. Snethen, M. Coate, and S. Merwin.[7] In 1809, the *Minutes* struck something of a compromise, listing the book agents in relation to the conference (New York) and above the districts. The *Minutes* privileged that special appointment above others. It listed the missionaries and the person traveling with the bishop (Henry Boehm for that year) in relation to a specific district, though without a circuit or station designation.[8]

The "special appointments" in American Methodism really institutionalized but divided offices held by Wesley. So several points:

- Special appointments structured offices or roles that Wesley played as, like his, connectional in nature and serving the whole.
- The century saw the gradual expansion of the number and character of these appointments.
- The church increasingly struggled to find ways to visualize such offices as central and connectional.
- Methodists perceived these offices as essentially connective for Methodism as a whole.
- Methodists also recognized that the office-holders belonged within the ordering structure for ministry, the conference, and in relation to the appointment and supervisory authority.
- Methodists knew that such offices needed a permanent home, a location.

CONNECTION AND ACCOUNTABILITY

Very early in its life, Methodism struggled with issues in reporting, accountability, and structure that the connectional or special appointment presented, given that its responsibilities, while general, required some location; that the special appointee remained within the itinerancy; and that oversight might need to be provided by persons also in the itinerancy. And, as annual conferences stabilized as geographically defined areas within which preachers held membership, connectional appointments seemed to require at once local, conference, and general dimensions. Visualizing that had posed problems for those crafting the *Minutes*, as we have seen.

What was unclear then, and has remained unclear to this day, was how best substantively and structurally to care for that connectional service, relation, accountability, and reporting. How were and how are those of us in "special" appointments to exercise those ministries in truly connectional but responsible fashion? How should they and we be connected and where should we report—on the most general level, primarily to the annual conference, or directly to local Methodism? (Or, as we shall ask in a final chapter, do such ministries deserve some new or refashioned structures that would better account for the multiple levels on which we serve the connection?)

To recap:

- In 1799 and 1801, the church achieved and represented the accountability as to the *connection as a whole* by depicting book agent or publisher Cooper with the bishops and those traveling with the bishops.
- In 1802, the *Minutes* displayed the accountability to *the conference* as primary by lodging Cooper immediately behind the presiding elder on the Philadelphia District.
- In 1804, the *Minutes* accented *local accountability* by visualizing the book agents as being on the circuit. In 1809, the *Minutes* again isolated the placement of the agents, but in relation to the New York Conference as a whole.[9]

In each of these depictions, the church understood persons in special appointments—the book agents, the missionaries, those traveling with the bishops—to be accountable at every Methodist level. But where would that primary accountability lie—to the general church, to the conference, to local Methodism?

OVERSIGHT

The issues of accountability and responsibility focused early on the matter of publishing. Indeed, the very first conference of American Methodism, that of 1773, sought to rein in Robert Williams's independent printing of Wesley's works and to bring publishing under Wesley's and the conference's authority.[10] Thereafter, early Methodism struggled to achieve a multilayered accountability with respect to what would be known as the Book Concern. Always the bishops, especially Francis Asbury, took a hand in its operations. Indeed, Asbury's supervision of publishing preceded the formal organization of the MEC and grew out of his long-term close relationship with John Dickins, the church's publisher or book agent from 1783 to 1798. Asbury moved Dickins from North Carolina to New York to take on the church's publishing, relocated him later to Philadelphia, and kept in regular touch with him, as his collected works and the history of the publishing house amply document.[11]

When Asbury persuaded the church to create a central authority to coordinate and streamline its decision making, this short-lived council made publishing its main business.[12] In its 1789 session, Asbury and the presiding elders (district superintendents), including Dickins, the "Council formed of the most experienced Elders in the Connexion" adopted an eight-point "Constitution," half of which governed procedure, the other half of which pertained to extension ministries:

3. To direct and manage all the Printings which may be done, from Time to Time, for the Use and Benefit of the Methodist Church in *America*.
4. To conduct the Plan of Education and manage all Matters which may, from Time to Time, pertain to any College or Houses built, or about to be built, as the Property of the Methodist Connexion.
5. To remove, or receive, and appoint the Salary of any Tutors, from Time to Time, employed in any Seminary of Learning belonging to the said Connexion.
6. In the Intervals of the Council, the Bishop shall have Power to act in all contingent Occurrences relative to the Printing Business, or the Education and Economy of the College.

The minutes then indicate, "After the Council had finished the Constitution as above; they then proceeded, with perfect Unanimity, to form the following Resolutions," the last and ninth of which read: "Considering the Weight of the Connexion, the Concerns of the College, and the Printing-Business; it is resolved that another Council shall be convened at *Baltimore*, on the First Day of *December*, 1790."

This next and last meeting devoted almost all of its business to extension ministries—publishing, education, missionaries, salaries, and pensions. The minutes bear citing in full:

Question. What Members are present?
Answer—*Francis Asbury, Bishop; Freeborn Garrettson, Francis Poythress, Nelson Reed, John Dickins, Philip Bruce, Isaac Smith, Thomas Bowen, James O. Cromwell, Joseph Everett, Charles Connoway.*

Quest. What power do this Council consider themselves *invested* with by their electors?
Ans. First, They *unanimously* consider themselves invested with *full* power to act *decisively* in all temporal matters: And, secondly, that of *recommending* to the several Conferences any new Canons, or alterations to be made in any old ones.

Quest. What can be done to promote the book-business?
Ans. 1, In every District where it is practicable, let some trusty diligent Preacher be appointed, as travelling *book-steward*, to preach, and supply the people with books. 2, In districts where this is not practicable, let every *Member* of the Council diligently recommend to the travelling Preachers, to exert themselves in promoting the sale of books. 3, Let every Member of the Council do what he can to forward his own books, or the books of other Preachers, to the Circuits for which they are designed. 4, Let every Member of the Council do what he can to collect and forward book-money, at least once in every three months, if any conveyance can be found, to *John Dickins*, Superintendent of the book-business.

Quest. Who are appointed as travelling book-stewards, by the order of the Council?
Ans. Philip Cox and *William Thomas.*

Quest. How shall such stewards be appointed for the future?

Ans. Any Preacher, being recommended by the presiding Elder and Conference of a district, as a proper person to act in such business, shall be appointed by the Council, when sitting; and, in the intervals of the Council, by the Bishops.

Quest. What can be done to procur religious experiences and letters for the *Arminian Magazine?*

Ans. Let those Members of the Council who choose it, write a *brief account* of their own experiences; and let all the Members procur such experiences and letters of other persons as appear to be unexceptionable, and send the whole to *John Dickins*, who shall submit it to the inspection of a Committee; and they shall have full power to *publish*, or *suppress*, as may be thought most proper.

Quest. Who shall form such a Committee?

Ans. Richard Whatcoat, Henry Willis, Thomas Haskins, and *John Dickins*, or any two of them.

Quest. What book shall be published in the course of the two following years?

Ans. The *Arminian Magazine;* the Rev. Mr. *Fletcher's Works; Hymn Books;* the *Saint's Rest;* the *Christian Pattern;* the *Primitive Physic;* the *Form of Discipline; Instructions for Children;* and the *Pamphlet on Baptism.* But the Bishops shall have a discretionary power of preparing the controversy for the Magazine, and publishing such tracts as *they* may think necessary for the benefit of the connexion: And *John Dickins* shall have a discretionary power of limiting the publications, according to the state of finances.

Quest. Shall we publish Mr. *Wesley's* 4 Volumes of Sermons, before the sitting of the next Council?

Ans. If our finances will admit of it, and a sufficient number of subscribers can be obtained.

Quest. What shall be done to support the credit and finish the building of *Cokesbury-College?*

Ans. In every Circuit, let a subscription be handed to such of our Members as are able and willing to contribute *One Dollar* per annum, as long as they think proper; and the subscriptions and money be brought to the several Conferences.

Quest. Can any thing *more* be done for *Cokesbury-College?*

Ans. Yes; the Council can obtain the loan of *One Thousand Pounds*, within the space of two years, which may be repaid at leisure, and without any interest—*Four Hundred Pounds* of which shall be applied to support the annual credit of the College; and the other *Six Hundred* to finish the building.

Quest. What is the expense of the Charity-boys, for the present year, in *Cokesbury-College?*

Ans. Upwards of *Three Hundred Pounds.*

Quest. Shall the Bishop have power to draw any money out of the book-profits, for the *partial* supply of any Church or Preacher that may be in pressing need?

Ans. By the recommendation of the Elder of a district, the Bishop may draw as far as *Three Pounds* per month; but no farther.

Quest. Who are the present Teachers in *Cokesbury-College?*

Ans. Jacob Hall, A.M. Teacher of Natural Philosophy, the Mathematics, Rhetorick and the Languages: *Patrick McCloskey,* Teacher of the *Greek* and *Latin* Languages, and the *English* Grammar: *Charles Tait,* Teacher of the *Latin.*

Quest. Can any thing be done to prevent the Students of *Cokesbury-College,* from *trafficking,* or *exchanging* their property with each other?

Ans. Yes: If any Student shall be detected in *selling* or *bartering* any of his property with another Student, without the consent of a Teacher, he shall be punished at the discretion of the Tutors.

Quest. As many of our Church are unfinished and in debt; and our grave-yards unfenced; what can be done for *their* relief?

Ans. First, let the Elders stir up the people to do all *they* can for their own Churches. Secondly, let Subscriptions, or public Collections, be made for the purpose.

Quest. As the Presiding Elders have only a *partial* supply at Quarterly-Meetings, to *whom* shall they present their annual accounts?

Ans. To the Bishop and Conference; where they shall receive a *proportion-able* supply of their deficiencies, according to the sum which may be brought to the Conference for *that* purpose.

Quest. As the Bishop is not supplied from the Circuits, to *whom* shall he render his account?
Ans. To the Council.

Quest. What shall be done if an opening should be made of settling a Teacher, or Preacher, among any of the *Indian Nations?*
Ans. The Bishop shall have liberty to draw a sum, not exceeding *Twenty-four Pounds* per annum, for that purpose.

Quest. What advice shall we give our brethren who desire to erect *District-Schools?*
Ans. 1, They may proceed in building such Schools, if they will collect money, within their respective districts, sufficient to begin and complete the buildings; and will also procure endowments of lands: But they shall receive no *assistance* from other districts. 2, We advise, that their economy should be established on the plan of *Cokesbury-College;* and the Teachers always appointed by the Bishop and Council. 3, The Schools shall be built as far *westward* as may be convenient, for the benefit of new settlements, and to procure *larger* endowments of lands. 4, When any such houses are founded, whatever subscriptions have been, or may be, taken for *Cokesbury-College*, shall then be applied to the proper use of any such *school* within the district where such money may be subscribed. 5, Whatever monies the Council may, from time to time, command for charitable purposes, shall then be divided between *Cokesbury-College* and such Schools, according to the number of children on charity, at the discretion of the Council.

Quest. What can be done towards the *relief* of our Preachers, who cannot obtain the Salaries allowed by our Canons?
Ans. 1, Let a Steward be appointed in *every* Society, whether large or small, who shall see collections made and brought to the General Stewards every Quarterly-Meeting. 2, Let the Canon, which requires the Stewards in case of deficiencies, to write circular-letters, be duly enforced; and every Preacher read such letters to the different Societies. 3, Let the cities, towns, and circuits, that are able, communicate with the poorer circuits.

Quest. Who shall be appointed to superintend the economy of the College, in the recess of the Council and the absence of the Bishop?
Ans. Nelson Reed, John Dickins, and Joseph Everett.

Quest. Who shall be appointed to inspect the Fasters bills, and make their payments?
Ans. Philip Rogers, Jeffe Hollingsworth, Samuel Owings, and *Emanuel Kent.*

Quest. As we think it primitive, prudent, and *decent,* that men and women should sit a-part in public congregations, what can be done to promote it amongst our people?
Ans. Let proper divisions be made in our houses; and, where it is practicable, let separate doors be made for the men and women, both white and black; and let all the Preachers keep special order at every meeting, according to the Canon in that case.

Quest. What money is *now* on hand, belonging to the Preachers' Fund?
Ans. One Hundred and Sixty-eight Pounds One Shilling and Four Pence.

Quest. What can be done to secure money, that may be collected for this purpose, in the future?
Ans. Let it be deposited in the Book-Fund, and draw lawful interest.

Quest. How shall money be drawn, from time to time, out of this Fund, for the relief of distressed Preachers?
Ans. When *such* a Preacher is recommended by a Conference, the Bishop shall immediately draw an order for books or money, to be obtained in any circuit or district.

Quest. As the Bishop complains, that some Preachers look to him for a supply of their deficiencies, what is the judgment of the Council in this case?
Ans. The Council judge it expedient to inform them, that the Bishop has *no Fund* for such supplies, any farther than is contained in these Minutes.

Quest. As *some* of the Members of Council complain of long and expensive journies, what can be done for their assistance in the future?
Ans. If the districts, on the extremities of the continent, from which some of the Members come, do not supply them, the Council, when able, shall bear their expences to and from the Council.

Quest. When and where shall the next Council be held?
Ans. At *Cokesbury-College* or *Baltimore,* on the first day of *December,* 1792.[13]

Asbury's prerogative of appointing the presiding elders (district superintendents) made the Council potentially a bishop-controlled operation and doomed it. In its stead, Methodism created the General Conference. This body, with its plenary authority, assumed oversight for publishing as well as other extension operations but it decided to meet only quadrennially. Such general oversight had, perforce, to be episodic and that exercised day to day by Asbury, at best epistolary. How could the church's interests in such delegated responsibilities be overseen day to day, week to week? Could some local body be designated to work along with the book agent or book agents? In 1796, General Conference[14] assigned oversight to the Philadelphia Conference and that body delegated the responsibility to the presiding elders of Philadelphia, a body of seven in 1797. The Philadelphia portion of the *Minutes* specified that new agency:

> Quest. 14. *What regulations have been made in respect to the Printing-Business, and the publication of books?*
> *Ans.* The Philadelphia conference, in whom the management of these affairs was invested by the general conference, and who have not time during their annual sittings to complete this business, have, by the advice and consent of Bishop Asbury, unanimously appointed the following persons to be a standing committee, viz.

> Ezekiel Cooper, *Chairman*

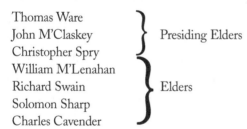

Thomas Ware
John M'Claskey   } Presiding Elders
Christopher Spry
William M'Lenahan
Richard Swain   } Elders
Solomon Sharp
Charles Cavender

> . . . [T]he general book-steward shall lay before the committee, all manuscripts, books, and pamphlets, which are designed for publication, except such as the general conference has authorized him to publish.[15]

When the Book Concern was moved back to New York, the same provision applied. The New York Conference assumed oversight and voted that "the stationed preachers in New York and Brooklyn be a committee on the

Book Concern."[16] Thus the church set a pattern of conference oversight of special ventures. Missions, colleges, theological schools, hospitals, and a variety of other ventures would be handled similarly.

Individual conferences, or several conferences together, would oversee efforts that served the connectional common good and would oversee those *specially* appointed to serve in these efforts. So, for instance, several conferences would together support and oversee colleges, and later seminaries, deemed to function connectionally or, at least, regionally. So sponsoring conferences looked after Wesleyan University in Connecticut, Randolph-Macon College in Virginia, Boston University, and the denomination's myriad colleges (male and female), sending visiting committees to oversee operations and report back.

CONFERENCES AS MEANS OF SUPERVISION

Educators, books agents, missionaries, heads of mission and other societies, fund-raisers and colporteurs, and eventually chaplains as ordained preachers had direct accountability to annual conferences in addition to whatever oversight was exercised by advisory or visiting committees. The array of extension ministries developed by the middle decades of the nineteenth century and conference responsibility for continuing oversight for the connection as a whole can be exhibited by the appointments in one of the larger, older conferences. The Philadelphia and New England conferences will serve to illustrate. By 1862 the former enjoyed the special responsibility of appointing and reviewing the character of the corresponding secretary of the missionary society (the nineteenth-century counterpart to general secretary), John P. Durbin. He was accountable to the North Philadelphia District and to the Trinity Quarterly Conference. The minutes listed three other persons with him for that district and below the regular appointments: A. Manship, agent of Philadelphia Conference Tract Society, member of Hedding Quarterly Conference; S. Higgins, Sunday school agent, member of Twelfth Street Quarterly Conference; and Jos. Welsh, chaplain of the 91st Regiment, P. V., member of Greet Street Quarterly Conference.[17] The South Philadelphia

District listed the president and a faculty member from Dickinson College and the chaplain to the Eastern State Penitentiary. The Snow Hill District listed in special connectional roles a missionary to India, the principal of Union Academy, and two chaplains. Wilmington, which previously had carried two faculty members of Wesleyan Female College, listed a chaplain, as did Reading and Easton.[18]

By 1865 the Philadelphia Conference listed more such appointments, the additions primarily as chaplains in the United States Army—one for N. Philadelphia, six for S. Philadelphia, one for Reading, three for Wilmington, one for Easton, two for Snow Hill.[19] For the New England Conference, the Boston District carried James Porter, assistant book agent, member of Hanover Street Quarterly Conference; Joseph Cummings, president of Wesleyan University, member of the Methodist General Bromfield Street Quarterly Conference; John W. Merrill, professor in Biblical Institute (soon to be renamed Boston Theological Seminary and to be incorporated into the newly established Boston University), member of North Russell Street Quarterly Conference; Lynn District listed two chaplains and William Butler, missionary to India. The Springfield District listed a chaplain, an agent of the American Bible Society, and Raymond Miner, then principal of Wilbraham Academy, later to be theologian for the church.[20]

What gave teeth to conference accountability? The review of character—a Methodist practice now rendered largely ceremonially and in collective fashion. In the nineteenth century, each and every one of the above "extension" ministers was subject to and subjected himself to the annual, personally administered scrutiny by his brethren. Methodism's premier mid-century historian/interpreter, Abel Stevens, explains:

> A usage exists in Methodist Conferences which is without a parallel, we believe, in any other ecclesiastical body. Every member, however venerable with piety and long service, is annually subjected to a sort of judicial examination; put under a virtual arrest, even though there may not be an intimation against his character. No exception is admitted, save that of the presiding officer, who is tried, in a similar manner, at the General Conference. The member thus under examination must stand frankly before

all his assembled brethren, any and all of whom may question him, or animadvert on his conduct. His faults, or even mannerisms, are deemed proper subjects of comment, and brotherly counsel; if they amount to vices, the inquiry is converted into a formal trial, and adjudicated according to the laws of the church. This is a severe discipline, and might seem oppressive; but it is self-imposed, it has the sanction of primitive usage, it gives a peculiar confidence, and even tenderness, to the mutual relations of Methodist preachers, and has been very salutary in preserving the purity of the ministry.[21]

Two entries in the minutes of the New England Conference reinforce Stevens's explanation:

After an excellent and refreshing prayer-meeting of an hour, the Conference resumed its *business*,—that is to say, the examination into the character sustained by every minister connected with the body, which is *the* work of an annual Methodist Conference, *par excellence*. Till this is done, the Conference cannot adjourn; and its presiding bishop is subject to arraignment for maladministration, if he fail to "call the name, or cause to be called, that of every preacher . . ."

In 1872 the secretary for that conference, with respect to the examination of character, recorded:

"Then came the fiery ordeal, to which every member of the body must be annually subjected, for all the years of his ecclesiastical life in the Methodist communion, . . ." and reported one complaint referred to "a committee of fifteen for trial."[22]

That same year, the head of Boston University School of Theology, soon to be the long-term president of the university as a whole, made explicit the application of the examination of character to what was then and remains to this day the most worrisome extension ministry category, namely, seminary faculty. In an important review of theological education in northern Methodism, William F. Warren noted the following checks on the-then three theological schools (Boston, Garrett, and Drew) and their faculties. I reproduce the whole list so that the reader can appreciate fully the importance of item 4 with respect to individual faculty members. Warren writes with regard to seminaries:

1. Each is officially placed under the direct supervision of the bishops of the Methodist Episcopal Church.
2. No professor can be appointed to any chair in either of the three institutions without the concurrence of the bishops.
3. In at least two of them no professor can take his chair until, in the presence of the Board of Trust, he have signed a solemn declaration, to the effect that so long as he occupies the same he will teach nothing inconsistent with the doctrines and discipline of the Methodist Episcopal Church.
4. At the *Annual Conference examination of character*, every professor—save one who chances to be a layman—is each year liable to arrest if even a rumor of heterodoxy is abroad against him.
5. Each institution is inspected, and its pupils annually examined as to what they have been taught, by visitors delegated from adjacent annual conferences.
6. Each has ecclesiastical qualifications affecting the appointment of trustees.
7. Each is required to report to every General Conference.[23]

I am confident that some United Methodists would love to see this program reinstituted. I am equally confident, based on long experience, that faculties would mightily resist such an effort. What needs to be noted here is that these accountability safeguards were disappearing even as Warren spoke.

AFTERWORD

In the 1870s Methodists changed the system in ways that, over the long haul, would erode the direct peer, local, and conference oversight of extension ministries. These changes deserve fuller discussion than can be provided here, though we return to them in several ways in the chapters that follow. Here need only be mentioned what pertains to accountability.

First, conferences gradually dampened the "fiery ordeal" of examination of character. It became routinized, and eventually ritualized, into a report by the presiding elder (district superintendent) as to whether he brought charges against any preachers on his district. A familiar refrain, "Nothing against the preachers on the . . . district," effectively signaled that oversight had moved from the annual conference into the office of presiding elder. Thus ended the bonding probing by close colleagues of one another's character and ministry, an examination that Warren saw as safeguarding faculty orthodoxy.

Second, in the 1870s the Methodist missionary, Sunday school, tract, church extension, and other societies—the domain of important extension ministries and the template for treatment of others—underwent a significant transformation (see chapter 4). They became corporations accountable to General Conference and no longer boards effectively governed by the directors resident in the agency's headquarters. The church achieved accountability at the connectional level at the cost of the more day-to-day interaction that is possible when an agency and its head reported to local directors. A couple of decades later the MEC achieved something comparable in creating the University Senate, thereby nationalizing what had been the more localized conference oversight of its colleges, universities, and (newly established) theological schools.

By the latter Disciplinary alterations, the extension ministries that served the connection as a whole—in the general boards or in educational institutions—lost peer, local, and conference oversight. The former, gradual erosion of real Disciplinary accountability in the examination of character removed peer, local, and conference oversight of ministers generally, including that of the extension types. The one change constitutionally, the other practically, altered fundamentally how extension ministers related to the connection and especially to conferences in which their membership nevertheless remained.

Both Charles Wesley's hymn and Peter's visionary outreach to the Gentiles from Caesarea recognize that the communion of saints will include difference, sometimes difference that outside the church causes friction, conflict, even war. So Wesley's verse bids us pray to the Triune God to increase our fellowship, knit us in the bond of peace, join each to each and all to God's Spirit. Such counsel seems to have informed the close relation and mutual accountability that early Methodists sustained between those in extension-type roles and those in regular itinerancy.

The church kept experimenting with the relational forms, replacing one reporting or accountability scheme with another that seemed an improvement. The changes just mentioned that distanced extension-type posts from the local and conference levels were seen as progress. A question for today is whether present-day United Methodism can find between regular and extension ministries structural and relation schemes that reach for the unity in the spirit of Peter's dream and Charles Wesley's verse.

—⁓—

APPENDIX

Dickins's Booklist 1791

The following Books are published by JOHN DICKINS, *NE 182, Race Street, near Sixth Street, Philadelphia; for the use of the Methodist Societies in the United States of America; and the profits thereof applied for the general benefit of the said Societies. Sold by the publisher, and the Ministers and Preachers in the several Circuits.*

The Arminian Magazine, Vol, 1st and 2d at 12*L*, [Shillings] per volume.
The Rev. Mr. Wesley's Notes on the New Testament in 3 vols. Well bound 17*L*
The same lettered 18*L* 6d [pence].
Thomas a Kempis, bound 2*L*
Primitive Physic, bound 3*L*
The Form of Discipline for the Methodist Church, with Treatises on Predestination, Perseverance, Christian Perfection, Baptism, &c. All bound together 3, 6d.
The Experiences of about twenty British Methodist Preachers, well bound and lettered 5*L*, 7d 1-2
The Experience and Travels of Mr. Freeborn Garrettson, well bound 3*L*
A Pocket Hymn-Book, containing three hundred Hymn well bound and lettered 3*L* 9*d*.
The Excellent works of the Rev. Mr. John Fletcher, published one volume at a time; the whole will contain about six volumes: the 1st and 2d vols. Now published, well bound and lettered at 5*L* 7d 1-2 per volume.

An Extract on Infant Baptism, stitched 9d.

Children's Instructions, stitched 6d.

An Abridgment of Mrs. Rowe's Devout Thoughts, bound *1L 10d* 1-2.

A Funeral Discourse on the death of that great Divine, the Rev. John Wesley, stitched 1.1d.

The Saints Everlasting Rest will be republished some time in Decem. 1791; well bound 5 *L* 7d 1-2.

Minutes of the Methodist Conferences, 4d.

As the profits of these books are for the general benefit of the Methodist Societies, it is humbly recommended to the Members of the said Societies, that they will purchase no books which we publish, of any other person than the aforesaid JOHN DICKINS, *or the Methodist Ministers and Preachers in the several Circuits, or such persons as sell them by their consent.*

2

Extension Ministers: Connectional Builders

I Corinthians 3:5-15

[5]What then is Apollos? What is Paul? Servants through whom you came to believe, as the Lord assigned to each. [6]I planted, Apollos watered, but God gave the growth. [7]So neither the one who plants nor the one who waters is anything, but only God who gives the growth. [8]The one who plants and the one who waters have a common purpose, and each will receive wages according to the labor of each. [9]For we are God's servants, working together; you are God's field, God's building.

[10]According to the grace of God given to me, like a skilled master builder I laid a foundation, and someone else is building on it. Each builder must choose with care how to build on it. [11]For no one can lay any foundation other than the one that has been laid; that foundation is Jesus Christ. [12]Now if anyone builds on the foundation with gold, silver, precious stones, wood, hay, straw—[13]the work of each builder will become visible, for the Day will disclose it, because it will be revealed with fire, and the fire will test what sort of work each has done. [14]If what has been built on the foundation survives, the builder will receive a reward. [15]If the work is burned up, the builder will suffer loss; the builder will be saved, but only as through fire.

—⚒—

I   Jesus, from whom all blessings flow,[1]
    Great builder of thy church below,
    If now thy Spirit moves my breast,
    Hear, and fulfil thine own request!

2 The few that truly call thee Lord,
And wait thy sanctifying word,
And thee their utmost Saviour own,
Unite, and perfect them in one.

3 O let them all thy mind express,
Stand forth thy chosen witnesses;
Thy power unto salvation show,
And perfect holiness below!

. . .

6 From every sinful wrinkle free,
Redeemed from all iniquity,
The fellowship of saints make known!
And, O my God, might I be one!

7 O might my lot be cast with these,
The least of Jesu's witnesses!
O that my Lord would count me meet
To wash his dear disciples' feet!

8 This only thing do I require:
Thou knowest 'tis all my heart's desire
Freely what I receive to give,
The servant of thy church to live;

9 After my lowly Lord to go,
And wait upon thy saints below;
Enjoy the grace to angels given,
And serve the royal heirs of heaven.

10 Lord, if I now thy drawings feel,
And ask according to thy will,
Confirm the prayer, the seal impart,
And speak the answer to my heart.

In chapter 1 we saw the emergence in American Methodism of special appointments to fill roles played by Wesley. Full attention to the task, a headquarters in or from which to operate, specialization and expertise, and ongoing involvement occasioned and demanded the creation of what would now be termed extension ministries. The church selected full members of the traveling connection as book agents, missionaries, faculty, heads of societies, and colporteurs and kept them closely tied on local, conference, and connectional levels. From the start, Methodism struggled with how best to provide the oversight that such delegation of authority and power represented. Over time, as a later chapter shows, both the structures of oversight and the nature of the special, or extension, roles evolved significantly. By the late twentieth century the most prominent of these "appointments beyond the local church"—those to general agencies—had become somewhat distant and bureaucratic and other such roles (chaplains, faculty members) marginal to conference life.

Earlier, I suggested that, by contrast, nineteenth-century extension ministries enjoyed considerable prominence on conference and local levels, as well as at the connectional level. Indeed, they played central leadership roles. This chapter chronicles such prestige, centrality, and importance in the careers of two persons who connected Methodism in their day: Nathan Bangs and John Price Durbin. Both lived the counsel of the apostle Paul and of Charles Wesley. As builders, innovators, and interpreters, each effectively connected a dynamically sprawling Methodism.

NATHAN BANGS (1778–1862)

Spokesperson, Editor

Known today as Methodism's premier early historian, Nathan Bangs shaped the story he then narrated. "No name is more fully identified with the history of American Methodism, for the last sixty years, than that of Nathan Bangs." So affirmed one younger, prominent contemporary and close observer of Methodist affairs, who continued: "His biography, when it comes to be fitly written, will be, to a large extent, a history of the Church."[2] If Bishop Asbury epitomized earlier Methodism, Bangs epitomized the next chapter. Bangs helps us grasp their distinctive offices. In treating the momentous year of 1816 in his history of the Methodist Episcopal Church, Bangs devoted almost thirty pages to an Asbury eulogy. He covered the bishop's last days, noted that he had died en route to General Conference, recalled his being disinterred for ceremonial reburial during General Conference in Baltimore's Light-street Church, and celebrated the distinguishing marks of his leadership and piety. After a long, detailed encomium, Bangs dared to note that even "the sun has its spots" and ventured "with great deference" two errors in the bishop's administration,[3] two infrastructural matters on which Asbury failed to encourage Methodist development or ensure its prosperity. The first had to do with "learning and a learned ministry," education and educational institutions, Methodism's intellectual self-promotion, and the church's place in and for culture, science, knowledge, and literature. The second had to do with support for ministry, ministers, and ministerial families and implicitly the great Asburian taboo, married itinerants. In Bangs's judgment, Asbury mistakenly had kept Methodism "aloof from the world," discouraging education so as to protect piety and discouraging property (churches and parsonages) so as to safeguard itinerancy. Such concerns recur through Bangs's narrative and constituted his life's work.[4]

Transitioning the Teaching Office

Connecticut-born, educated in village schools, a teacher before his conversion and call, Bangs saw that Methodism faced competition on a flank that Asbury had not adequately protected.[5] What were Methodism's imperatives for Bangs? Hold on to those convicted of sin in camp meeting or revival! Nurture after converting! Bring up the children baptized in the faith! Sustain itself in the east even as it itinerated west! Create media, church structures, and institutions for formation, education, advocacy, and transmission!

The message was clear: Methodism should look to its self-preservation and therefore establish practices, policies, resources, buildings, and connectional systems that would hold members in the church as frontier gave way to farming community, crossroads to villages and towns, and struggling circuits to robust congregations. Bangs knew whereof he spoke. Having settled in Canada to teach in 1799, he began itinerating in 1801 and was admitted on trial with a typically terse notation: "Recommended from Niagara Circuit 2 Years in Experience, pious travelled 9 Months approved, useful, clear—received."[6] He served successive frontier appointments in Upper Canada and Quebec and then districts of the New York Conference before being sent to the Albany District in 1808.

Bangs then held successive term appointments as presiding elder, as preacher in New York, and again as presiding elder before being elected book agent in 1820. The New York Conference elected him secretary in 1811, sent him repeatedly to General Conference, beginning with the first delegated General Conference (*MEA* 1812a), and would thereafter call on him for or appoint him to almost every task that required study or statement.[7] For instance, in 1827 at Troy, the Conference put him first on committees of three or four to "prepare an address to our people," to investigate a charge of ministerial malfeasance, to oversee the missionary cause, to revise the course of study, and to provide oversight for the Colonization Society. He led the conference from the floor, put forward various motions, and was confirmed in his leadership by being elected to General Conference (apparently second). The next year, Bangs made a motion requesting a funeral sermon for Freeborn Garrettson, was put first of three on a committee to write Garrettson's memoirs, was appointed by the bishop to preach the funeral sermon, offered a motion dealing with masonry, and was appointed to small committees to consider missions, matters relating to Wesleyan University, and compliance with Disciplinary strictures on pew sales and rentals.[8]

From such conference leadership posts and comparably responsible ones on a national level, Bangs participated actively in building and promoting Methodism's sociocultural-missional infrastructure. He was perhaps Methodism's most visible figure between the death of Bishop Francis Asbury and the Civil War leader Bishop Matthew Simpson. Elected to the office of book agent, he assumed responsibility for the publishing enterprise of the church, undertook the editing of the newly established *Methodist Magazine*, exercised the leading role in creating the *Christian Advocate*, championed important causes like missions and education (indeed, crafted their warranting, authorizing, and constituting documents), and assumed authority to interpret signal Methodist events and developments.

His posts as editor gave Bangs a connection-wide and unparalleled voice. The entire church read his words and those of subsequent *Advocate* and magazine editors—most prominently, John McClintock, Thomas E. Bond, Matthew Simpson, Daniel Curry, William Nast, J. B. McFerrin, Daniel B. Whedon, Thomas O. Summers, Abel Stevens, J. J. Tigert, J. M. Buckley, J. R. Joy, and Nolan B. Harmon.[9] The editors' voice proved more available, regularized, permanent, uniform, and influential than anyone else's in the church, including that of the itinerating bishops (McKendree, George, Roberts, and successors). To be sure, like the field preaching, "oral" Wesley, the bishops received an eager hearing where and when Methodists assembled in conference or camp. However, the editors—the American "print" Wesley—could be read everywhere, again and again, and their opinions passed from subscriber to family, friends, class members, and prospective converts.

The voice of Methodist publishing was heard; indeed, as we note below, it had already succeeded in creating a textually defined national Wesleyan community, putting into hands and homes the church's witness in verse, narrative, doctrine, and discipline. Texts transmitted, inculcated, converted, and sustained. They modeled, bonded, ritualized, disciplined, and set boundaries. Methodism had been the first to establish a publishing house and to center its evangelical and evangelistic mission by marketing Wesleyan materials. Gradually, what began as a business to reprint the received Wesleyan (British) message and to transmit official American (MEC) actions began to shape the witness and thereby an increasingly connection-wide textual community.[10]

Bangs contributed actively to this subtle transfer of connectional intellectual leadership and community. His effectiveness as official spokesperson earned him other teaching office responsibilities in successive General Conferences: head of Methodist missions; president of Wesleyan University (briefly); denominational apologist and historian; presiding elder; and episcopal candidate.

In the fast-growing church in the expanding new nation, the teaching office, exercised by Wesley and attempted by Asbury, slipped away from the bishops. It did so legally through General Conference's formal claim to speak for the church, albeit at four-year intervals. It did so programmatically and week to week through the communicative effectiveness of other teachers—first the editors, then the colleges, and eventually the general agencies. However, the episcopal office remained the most prestigious that the church could bestow and so Methodism recognized the significance of these teaching offices and officers by electing them bishops. Bangs did not pursue the episcopacy as avidly as his immediate predecessor and his successors who were elected bishops: Joshua Soule, John Emory, and Beverly Waugh.[11] Later the church would elevate to the episcopacy college presidents, and agency heads, ironically both recognizing a teaching office distinct from episcopacy and removing persons from it.

An American Methodist Voice and Identity

Bangs established himself as Methodist spokesperson with apologetical works that appeared in 1815, 1816, 1817, and 1820: *The Errors of Hopkinsianism Detected and Refuted; The Reformer Reformed; An Examination of the Doctrine of Predestination;* and *A Vindication of Methodist Episcopacy.*[12] These books, along with others like Asa Shinn's *An Essay on the Plan of Salvation* of 1813, defended Wesleyan theology and Methodist ministry, orders, and episcopacy against the church's most powerful critics. In the first three, Bangs responded to Calvinists who derided Methodism's thought and in the last to Episcopalians who questioned its ecclesial legitimacy.[13]

In confronting the Calvinists, Bangs picked up where Fletcher left off. With his anti-Calvinist works, particularly *The Errors of Hopkinsianism Detected and Refuted* and *The Reformer Reformed*, Bangs made the case for hallmark Methodist doctrines of prevenient grace, human responsibility and freedom, holiness, and moral agency against Samuel Hopkins and other consistent Calvinists, who represented the premier American theological legacy—that of Jonathan Edwards. He produced these two works with the formal approval of the New York Conference.[14] His theological statements and the normative works on the Course of Study, thereafter obligatory for those entering ministry, addressed the concerns raised by the Committee of Safety at the 1816 General Conference:

> [T]hat, in some parts of the connexion, doctrines contrary to our established articles of faith, and of dangerous tendency, have made their appearance among us, especially the ancient doctrines of *Arianism, Socinianism* and *Pelagianism* . . .[15]

Bangs continued to explain, advocate for, and defend Methodist doctrine, practices, and orders in book-length publications, as for instance in *An Original Church of Christ: or, A Scriptural Vindication of the Orders and Powers of the Ministry of the Methodist Episcopal Church* (1837). He did as well throughout his four-volume *History of the Methodist Episcopal Church* (1838–41). He became the authoritative voice of the church through his editorial role and through the innovations he brought to Methodist publishing.

The Book Concern

Bangs assumed the role of book agent in 1820, with the active involvement of the New York Conference and a conference oversight committee, receiving that year what had been General Conference's authority: to authorize new publications. In 1818, at General Conference's behest, Joshua Soule launched the *Methodist Magazine*, authorized as *The Methodist Missionary Magazine* and variously titled thereafter (*Methodist Magazine and Quarterly Review, Methodist Quarterly Review, Methodist Review, Religion in Life, Quarterly Review*), a venture that the church sustained for almost two centuries. As Soule's successor Bangs gave American Methodism its national voice, *his* voice. "Nathan Bangs—Man of the Hour, Man of the Age" and his era "Years of the American Dream: The 1820's," James Pilkington judged, in the authoritative study of Methodist publishing. By contrast he labeled the pre-Bangs period "The Little Years: 1798–1820."[16] Bangs made the *Methodist Quarterly Review* (*MQR*) and the Book Concern.

Bangs transformed what had been essentially a distributing operation for British reprints and official denominational publications (*Minutes, Disciplines, Hymnbooks*) into a full-fledged publishing house capable of its own printing and binding. He expanded the serious and popular adult fare, entered the tract market, established Sunday school literature, added serials for children and youth to a diet previously limited to Wesley's *Catechism*, and effectively Americanized the Book Concern. He built, of course, on the work of his predecessors and contended from the start with regional competition that shared the innovative and Americanizing task. The greatest achievement of the Bangs years, for instance, the launching of what would be the newspaper with the widest national readership, the *Christian Advocate*, capitalized on earlier efforts: *New England Missionary Magazine*, 1815, edited by Martin Ruter (New Hampshire); *Western Christian Monitor*, 1816, edited by William Beauchamp (Ohio); *Zion's Herald*, 1823, edited by Barber Badger (Boston, and continuing to the present); and *Wesleyan Journal*, 1825, edited by William Capers (Charleston). Initially, the several regional efforts converged, with the *Wesleyan Journal* and *Zion's Herald* merging with the *Christian Advocate*.

The immediate and national success of the *Christian Advocate*—5,000 copies of the first issue, 25,000 subscribers in two years—made it a vital authoritative Methodist voice and the most widely distributed periodical in the world.[17] Coincidentally, its importance derived in part from continuing competition with regional and reforming impulses. Even as—indeed, even before—the *MQR* and *Advocate* claimed connectional prerogatives, resistance to centralized power and authority took literary and serial form.

Heading Sunday School and Missionary Initiatives

The *Advocates* constituted but one aspect of the Book Concern's advance into popular literature. It also became the engine for the church's evangelistic and missionary enterprise and for its dramatic expansion into popular nurture and family care. Methodism started with the adults, producing cheap tracts for the Methodist Tract Society, formed in 1817. In 1823, Bangs launched the *Youth's Instructor and Guardian*, a monthly aimed at youth and families and featuring woodcut illustrations. And, in 1827, when Methodists disengaged from the American Sunday School Union to constitute their own agency, Bangs established the *Child's Magazine* and increased the overall production of Sabbath instruction materials.

With its now-muscular media, Methodism capitalized readily and programmatically on the new theological, pedagogical, and psychological theory. In April 1827, deciding not to subsume its work in the Calvinist-dominated American Sunday School Union, the MEC founded the Sunday School Union of The Methodist Episcopal Church (SSU). They based it in New York City, with Nathan Bangs, critic of Calvinism and head of the Methodist Book Concern, as corresponding secretary.[18] The next year, General Conference endorsed the SSU and the *Discipline* specifically commended Sunday schools in every pastoral appointment.[19] The mandate hardly seemed necessary. A year's time had produced 251 auxiliary societies, 1,025 Sunday schools, 2,048 Sunday school superintendents, 10,290 teachers, and 63,240 students. Bangs explained the cause, promoted the Sunday school, and provided teacher-training counsel in a new regular feature of the ever more widely circulated weekly *The Christian Advocate*.

Bangs played a similar initiating and leadership role in missions. In 1819, under Bangs's leadership, the church established a missionary society to provide "pecuniary aid . . . to enable the Conferences to carry on their missionary labours on a more extended plan" and "to extend the influence of divine truth, by means of those missionaries which may, from time to time, be approved and employed by the Bishops and Conferences for that purpose."[20] Bangs served as the new society's principal head and promoter in early years, the drafter of its reports through 1837, and thereafter "resident corresponding secretary" until 1844. In fact, wherever and whatever Methodism did things organizationally Bangs seemed to be a part of it (among the prominent male Methodist figures who regularly attended

Phoebe Palmer's Tuesday Meetings for the Promotion of Holiness, along with bishops Edmund S. Janes and Leonidas Hamline and fellow educators Stephen Olin and John Dempster). After a short and largely unsuccessful stint as president of Wesleyan University (1841–42), Bangs returned to the regular ranks of the itinerancy, serving as pastor and presiding elder for the next decade. Though he was an important innovator, he was but one of a number of innovators and builders functioning in posts that we would now designate as "extension."

JOHN PRICE DURBIN (1800–1876)

Under bishops Francis Asbury and Thomas Coke the church launched an American Kingswood, a college for the infant movement called "Cokesbury College." Cokesbury failed; and the bishops' dream of schools for Methodism materialized only after both had died—Coke in 1814 and Asbury in 1816. The General Conferences of 1820 and 1824 charged annual conferences with the establishment of schools, literary institutions, and colleges, and permitted them to staff these institutions with conference members (not obliging them to "locate"). The imperative led to the creation of some ninety secondary-level institutions. Gradually, conferences, often collaboratively, also launched collegiate institutions, beginning with Augusta College in Kentucky (1822), followed by Randolph-Macon College in Virginia (1830), and Wesleyan University in Connecticut (1831). The first women's college, Wesleyan in Georgia, was approved and chartered in 1836.[21] By the Civil War Methodism had established, or was affiliated with, some two hundred such institutions. Many of these institutions were poorly funded, staffed, supported, and attended and did not survive long. By one estimate Methodism succeeded in establishing thirty-four "permanent" colleges before 1861.[22]

Conference-level oversight held the new colleges to Methodist values and expectations and bound them to the connection. Augusta, for instance, derived from the initiatives of the Ohio and Kentucky conferences in 1821. Leadership came from both conferences, Ohio contributing the first president, Martin Ruter, who came to the office from the helm of *Western Christian*

Advocate, and also John P. Durbin. The latter would go on to edit *The Christian Advocate* and from there to occupy the presidency of Dickinson College. And that college, taken over by the Methodists, enjoyed the sponsorship of Methodism's two strongest conferences, Baltimore and Philadelphia. Keeping conference and college close and the institution viable was the special charge of the presidents. And they, Durbin as a case in point, exhibited the connectional importance of the extension ministry, the strong ties with Methodism at the grassroots level, and the vitality of their place firmly and visibly within the life of the annual conference.

John Durbin, Educator

If Asbury epitomizes the first, aural/event/episcopal phases of Methodist connectionalism and Bangs that of press and voluntary society, Durbin represents a college phase and the foundation-laying for corporate management.[23] Born in 1800 of Methodist parents in Bourbon County, Kentucky, Durbin was apprenticed as a cabinet-maker at fourteen. At eighteen he experienced conversion and about the same time a call to preach. Accepted into membership one week and licensed to preach the next, he was immediately sent to the Limestone Circuit. In 1820, when the Western Conference was divided, he went with Ohio. He began his education in the 1820s during appointments, responding to the tutelage of several senior itinerants, including Martin Ruter, whom he would join later at Augusta. The image of the circuit rider reading on circuit, Wesley-like, may be mostly myth. Durbin gave reality to the myth. He started with the requisites—Wesley's and Fletcher's works, Clarke's Commentary—went on to grammar, Latin, and Greek and eventually enrolled formally as a college student. He attended Miami University while appointed in that vicinity, and Cincinnati College while there, graduating finally with an MA degree. Soon thereafter Durbin was made professor of ancient languages at Augusta College. He held that position for a few years, relinquishing it for health reasons, only to continue as agent for the college, in effect the itinerating admissions and development officer.

Durbin served briefly as chaplain of the United States Senate and also for a short time as editor of the *Christian Advocate* (New York). In 1834, he became principal (president) of Dickinson College, a post he held until 1845.[24] He transferred to the Philadelphia Conference in 1836 and eight times earned the conference's token of highest respect: election to represent it at General Conference. Five of those times he led the delegation, the highest accolade that conferences then (or now) accord their own.[25] Philadelphia turned to him at every point. The 1845 Conference appointed or elected him to preach the Conference Sermon (for 1846). Also he served as examiner in the Committees for Examination of the second-year exam on the "Bible as to ordinance or Sacraments."[26] Durbin also headed the Visiting Committee to Dickinson College in 1846 (the agency through which the church exercised its oversight of institutions).[27] In 1849, the bishop concurred in the conference's high estimation of J. P. Durbin and made him presiding elder of North Philadelphia.[28] A year later, in 1850, Durbin succeeded Charles Pitman as secretary of the Missionary Society.[29] He would make that perhaps the most important leadership position in the church, as we note below.

Durbin's prominence during his presidency at Dickinson and his overall career well symbolize the nature of the college–church relationship and also what served to connect Methodism at this juncture. If Asbury-the-bishop incarnated Methodist connectionalism in the early years and Bangs-the-editor in the early nineteenth century, then Durbin-the-president incarnated connectionalism for the pre–Civil War decades.[30] Durbin and his college president colleagues quite literally knit the church together on education's behalf. From the 1830s to the Civil War, colleges constituted the church's primary benevolence, the focus of its efforts at social and cultural uplift, its training ground for ministry, its center for inquiry and theologizing, and the agency through which the church exercised the teaching office.

Into the colleges the church poured its (limited) financial resources. On their behalf the emerging lay elites began to take leadership roles. There the church equipped its ministry, with Wesleyan, Dickinson, and Randolph-Macon serving, in effect, as the seminaries of their day. Through the colleges the church would carry on its larger mission of reforming the nation, joining with other denominations in common endeavor to instill Protestant commitment, republican ideals, and civic virtue in the nation's rising leaders.

John Durbin, Mission Head

Symbolizing, leading, and envisioning Methodism's mission to Christianize the nation—indeed, the world—was the office of the Missionary Society of the Methodist Episcopal Church and of its head, the corresponding secretary. In 1850, Durbin assumed that post.[31] Already prominent within his conference, and respected across the denomination, Durbin put new Disciplinary expectations into operation and perhaps more than any other individual transformed missions from a voluntary endeavor into a denominational enterprise. He did so while sustaining his close relations with annual conferences and the Methodist people.

The Philadelphia Conference *Minutes* registered Durbin's special appointment—"Cor. Sec. of Miss. Soc. of M. E. Church"—and carried the new national or denominational extension ministry role under the North Philadelphia District.[32] Through him, the Philadelphia Conference and its people had a very personal and direct connection to the mission enterprise. Durbin found a way of making missions a personal involvement for other conferences as well.

Durbin began his new work with a fresh vision of what conferences might be and do in missions and set out immediately to make conferences a more significant instrument in the missionary cause. His efforts (really endeavors to translate the *Discipline*'s mandates into conference operations) came apparently too late to catch the 1850 meeting of the Philadelphia annual conference. They drew responses elsewhere. For instance, the Troy Conference for 1850 passed an eight-point program, one apparently outlined in a communiqué from Durbin. It called for missionary organization at every level, for annual missionary meetings, for appointed collectors in "every class or neighborhood," and for reports and publication of the amounts collected—all muscled by the presiding elders who were to meet with the preachers and preach on missions.[33]

Other conferences passed very similar sets of programs for missions, often with some such introduction as "The Committee to whom was referred the papers from Dr. Durbin, Corresponding Secretary of the Missionary Society of the M.E. Church, presented their report, which was adopted . . ."[34] Each conference seemed to configure the program to suit its own taste. But they typically included the above ingredients, often adding an item that Troy omitted and that must have been part of Durbin's program, namely, to promote *The Missionary Advocate* within the conference.[35] The following year Philadelphia got on the program. It adopted a "Report of Committee on Missions," which called for a nine-point program: (1) monthly missionary prayer meetings or lectures in each church; (2) promotion of "our *Missionary Advocate*"; (3) annual missionary collections in November or December; (4) appointment of local missionary collectors; (5) publication annually of donors, collectors, and officers; (6) establishment of a missionary sermon at conference and holding of the anniversary during conference; (7) use of the Sunday schools as "a powerful auxiliary to the Missionary cause"; (8) their formal organization as auxiliaries where feasible; and (9) the creation of the category of life membership in the denominational society, a recommendation that the conference made to "the Parent Society."[36] By then, Philadelphia had further incentive for missionary enthusiasm. In addition to Durbin at the helm, it boasted two missionaries from its ranks: J. Calder, missionary to China, and D. D. Lore, missionary to Buenos Aires.[37]

In time, the deployment, staffing, and networking that Durbin specified and encouraged led to considerable expansion of extension roles, especially on conference levels, where the church's action took place. Hence the wisdom in Durbin's involvement of conferences beyond his own. In 1852, Durbin and the Missionary Society pushed a revised Constitution through General Conference and the New York legislatures. Among other things, it provided for Board, rather than New York Conference, responsibility for removal or replacement of the corresponding secretary between sessions of General Conference. It also allowed each annual conference a "vice-president from its own body."[38] Also, by this point the Missionary Society had recognized the strategic value of moving its annual meetings out of New York to convene around the connection, Philadelphia already having been the first of the alternative anniversary meeting sites, followed by Boston and Buffalo.[39]

In 1856, Philadelphia passed a resolution of approbation for African colonization, calling for sermons and a collection "on or about the 4th of July." By this point as well, the conference, in establishing what was becoming an increasingly complex committee structure, gave missions unusual prominence by appointing as its members "The Presiding Elders."[40] By that point, complexity, order, priority, regimen, reporting, and numbers had become important to Methodists. And conferences displayed their concerns with elaborate statistics and their values with money. By 1859, Philadelphia needed two committees to deal with missions, one with that title, another titled "Missionary Statistics." And, appropriately, conference projected for itself in the future a "Plan of Statistics for Annual Minutes," a thirteen-item report expected of each charge, including the "Missionary Report for Philadelphia Conference."[41] Thereafter, the *Minutes* showed very clearly just how each circuit and station performed on this and other points of religious vitality.

As Methodism embroiled itself in the Civil War, missions competed for conference attention with matters of loyalty, support for the war effort, supplying of chaplains, stands on slavery, and the like. By that time, with women having invested significantly in their own missionary society, support for missions took on more of a social character. In 1862, the Philadelphia Conference, still an all-male and clergy-only affair, featured a whole set of "Anniversaries"—annual meetings set to coincide with or follow conference. Sometimes these were evening affairs, such as with the Female Bible Society of the MEC, the Philadelphia City Home Mission, the Young Men's Central Home Mission, the Philadelphia Conference Tract Society, and the Philadelphia Conference Missionary Society. Including laity as well as clergy, women as well as men, these affairs transacted necessary business, heard annual reports, and featured multiple addresses.[42] Speakers would often be the key denominational players in the cause of the day; for missions that would be the conference's own John Durbin.

At the end of the war, northern Methodism geared up for larger conquests, a capital campaign among them. Clearly, missions also claimed the church's heart. That was made most visible, perhaps, by the new priority the Conference Missionary Society had in conference affairs. For starters, beginning in 1867, Durbin's Philadelphia Conference published the *Annual Report of the Missionary Society* as part of its own *Minutes* and numbered it sequentially.[43] The *Minutes* also gave a new prominence to the Society, listing its officers second after the stewards among the conference bodies. Two years later the Mission Society would stand first. The presiding elders still served as the standing committee on missions.

The 1867 conference, meeting in Harrisburg, took such symbolic gestures seriously. It heard fraternal addresses from other denominations, notably the The African Methodist Episcopal Church Zion (AMEZ), the Presbyterian Church, and the Lutheran Church, and introduced members of other denominations. It welcomed an invitation to "visit the rooms of the Young Men's Christian Association."[44] It received communiqués from the various denominational agencies and responded appropriately. It invited the members of the U.S. Senate and House of Representatives, then in session, to sit with it, and welcomed the reciprocal invitation to hold services in the House. It passed various resolutions, including one dispatched to the U.S. Senate and House.

Missions claimed further ritual gesture. J. B. McCullough, "appointed at the last session to preach the Annual Missionary Sermon before the Conference," did so to "marked attention." That evening, the fifth night of its meeting, the conference celebrated the Missionary Society's anniversary, completely packing "with ladies and gentlemen" the Locust St. Methodist Episcopal Church (the site for the conference as a whole). After opening devotions and the treasurer's report, the Reverend S. Pancoast of Upper Iowa spoke. The society then sang "From Greenland's Icy Mountains." Next, the Reverend Doctor De Hass of the Metropolitan Church, Washington, addressed the gathering. After a hymn, Dr. Durbin spoke and "sketched the field of missions as it now exists and is occupied by the M.E. Church, in an elaborate and eloquent manner, for which he is so peculiar." The assembly then nominated and elected the board of managers for the following year and were dismissed.[45]

The next day, "J. P. Durbin addressed the Conference in behalf of the Missionary Cause." Following his speech, the conference resolved "that the Missionary Cause in the future, as in the past, shall hold the first place in our affections, and that we hereby pledge ourselves to do our full part in paying any indebtedness that may be incurred by our Parent Board in maintaining our Missionary work at home and abroad." The conference then passed a resolution thanking "Bro. McCullough" for his missionary sermon and requesting a copy for publication.[46]

Another ritual action focused attention away from leaders and the pulpit and on every member. When passing the character of its members—the annual review by and through which the church assessed and guaranteed orthodoxy, effectiveness, integrity, and conformity—the conference did so with an interesting formula: "The names of all the effective Elders on this District were called, their collections reported, and their character passed."[47] This action, which connected approval of the individual's standing as a minister to his charge's collections, put into dramatic form what the *Minutes* and *Report* accomplished by table and statistic. It identified the mission of every station and circuit with what it contributed. It made clear that holding "the Missionary Cause . . . first . . . in our affections" meant organizing Methodism around collections. Missions, once the activity of conferences, had become a benevolence.

In 1868, Philadelphia recognized the half-century of Durbin's service by a motion "requesting J. P. Durbin, D.D., to preach a semi-centennial sermon at our next session," a motion "adopted by a rising vote."[48] It was a fitting tribute to Durbin. He had made Methodist missions effective by harnessing the main engine of Methodist life—the annual conference—to the missionary cause. By 1872, when Philadelphia elected him again and for the last time to General Conference and General Conference would reorganize its agencies (see chapter 4), missions stood first in conference affections. The *Minutes* registered its centrality with a new title page, *Minutes of the Eighty-Fifth Session of the Philadelphia Annual Conference of the Methodist Episcopal Church, Convened at St. Paul's M. E. Church, Philadelphia, Pa. Together with the Missionary Report.* The sessions brimmed with action about or statements concerning missions. Conferences had indeed responded to the overtures that Durbin had made in 1850.

At the General Conference that year, Durbin did not stand for reelection to the helm of the Missionary Society. He took a timely departure. The same conference, as we shall see in a later chapter, passed enabling legislation effectively transforming all its agencies from voluntary societies into denominational agencies. General Conference did so by making their boards, not just the corresponding secretary, elective by and accountable to itself. From this action flowed the eventual nationalization and centralization of denominational enterprise. Though the full development of bureaucracy would take some time, like other denominational endeavors, missions would increasingly be run from the top. Durbin's career and the Philadelphia Conference (over his nearly fifty-year association with it) illustrate the earlier chapter in extension ministries and the mission saga—one in which the church depended upon annual conferences to do its work, in which extension ministry figured prominently in conference life, and in which agency head and conference worked effectively together on connectional endeavors.

AFTERWORD

Nathan Bangs and John Price Durbin lived the counsel of Charles Wesley's hymn and that offered by Paul to the Corinthians. For their day they embodied and actualized Methodist connectionalism. As extension ministers (in today's parlance), they built, innovated, communicated, interpreted, and connected on behalf of a dynamically sprawling and centrifugally expanding Methodist system of itinerancy and conferences. They did so benefiting from those who had planted and watered before them and, of course, conscious that God gave the growth. They built on foundations others had laid and laid foundations for others, conscious that through them God builds the church. But build the church, create connectional structures, and establish missional infrastructure they did.

Whether we accent the agricultural or construction metaphor, we need to see that these extension ministries functioned in their planting and building in close connection with and in and through the conference system. The Bangses and Durbins succeeded because they lived and labored collaborating with their peers in ministry.

3

Chaplains

Ephesians 6:10-20

[10]Finally, be strong in the Lord and in the strength of his power. [11]Put on the whole armor of God, so that you may be able to stand against the wiles of the devil. [12]For our struggle is not against enemies of blood and flesh, but against the rulers, against the authorities, against the cosmic powers of this present darkness, against the spiritual forces of evil in the heavenly places. [13]Therefore take up the whole armor of God, so that you may be able to withstand on that evil day, and having done everything, to stand firm. [14]Stand therefore, and fasten the belt of truth around your waist, and put on the breastplate of righteousness. [15]As shoes for your feet put on whatever will make you ready to proclaim the gospel of peace. [16]With all of these, take the shield of faith, with which you will be able to quench all the flaming arrows of the evil one. [17]Take the helmet of salvation, and the sword of the Spirit, which is the word of God.

[18]Pray in the Spirit at all times in every prayer and supplication. To that end keep alert and always persevere in supplication for all the saints. [19]Pray also for me, so that when I speak, a message may be given to me to make known with boldness the mystery of the gospel, [20]for which I am an ambassador in chains. Pray that I may declare it boldly, as I must speak.

1   Soldiers of Christ, arise,[1]
       And put your armour on,
   Strong in the strength which God supplies
       Through his eternal Son;
       Strong in the Lord of hosts,
       And in his mighty power,
   Who in the strength of Jesus trusts
       Is more than conqueror.

2   Stand then in his great might,
       With all his strength endued,
   But take, to arm you for the fight,
       The panoply of God;
       That having all things done,
       And all your conflicts passed,
   Ye may o'ercome through Christ alone,
       And stand entire at last.

3   Stand then against your foes,
       In close and firm array;
   Legions of wily fiends oppose
       Throughout the evil day;
       But meet the sons of night,
       But mock their vain design,
   Armed in the arms of heavenly light,
       Of righteousness divine.

4   Leave no unguarded place,
       No weakness of the soul,
   Take every virtue, every grace,
       And fortify the whole;
       Indissolubly joined,
       To battle all proceed;
   But arm yourselves with all the mind
       That was in Christ, your Head.

As a prefiguring of the office of chaplain Methodists can look back to the early leader (almost bishop) and missionary to New England Jesse Lee (1758–1816). He was drafted during the Revolution[2] and recalled: "[As] a Christian and as a preacher of the gospel I could not fight. I could not reconcile it to myself to bear arms, or to kill one of my fellow creatures; however I determined to go, and to trust the Lord." He refused a gun, was put under guard and interrogated for his refusal to bear arms. He responded, "I could not kill a man with a good conscience, but I was a friend to our country, and was willing to do any thing that I could, while I continued in the army, except that of fighting." He served then as a noncombatant, continued preaching, and, in effect, played chaplain roles.[3]

Methodists did not emulate Lee's example to any significant extent until the Civil War effectively established the chaplaincy as a military and religious office. Before that point the United States had not needed or wanted the post. Indeed, as part of a money-saving effort in 1818, Congress actually eliminated the position for a couple of decades, along with those of army surgeons and judge advocates. Although the office had been restored and there were a few chaplains on staff in 1846 when the Mexican War broke, they were not mobilized. Nine ministers volunteered to serve as chaplains, only four of whom were Protestant.[4] The Civil War, however, created a huge demand and opportunity for chaplains. And by 1844, when the church split between North and South, Methodism had recognized chaplains as among the "special" appointments not subject to the rule of two-year appointments.[5]

Although some Methodists, like Quakers and like Lee earlier, proclaimed their pacifism and although early sentiment about the war was quite mixed— especially in the border states where both pro-slavery and free-soil sentiments contended—many, perhaps most, eventually supported either the Confederate or the Union cause. A few preachers took up arms. Many more volunteered in one of several chaplains' roles. In doing so, they enjoyed the fervid investment of annual conferences, again illustrating the close connection between such "extension" ministries and the regular itinerancy.

Chaplaincy, Confederate Style

As state after state seceded, as the Confederate States of America formed, and as war began, Southern Methodists (The Methodist Episcopal Church, South, and The Methodist Protestant Church [MECS and MPC])—some of whom opposed, some of whom championed secession—came first cautiously, then increasingly, to speak and preach about the new nation and the war. Despite several decades of commitment to spirituality and neutrality and despite explicit counsel from the Southern bishops to stay above the fray and deplore "the too extensive influence of the war spirit among our preachers," some editors, conferences, and individual ministers began to preach patriotism as a religious duty, the Confederate cause as ordained by God, and the aim of the war as independence.[6] Such sermonic and editorial endorsements (the MECS General Conference did not meet during the war and therefore offered no official church position) helped the South garner popular support and recruit Methodists into the Confederate army. Methodist preachers both acted out and voiced their support, volunteering as regular soldiers and non-combatants and as chaplains, some seventy-two of the ordained being appointed as officers or in the enlisted ranks in 1861 alone.[7]

Endorsements came also on official levels. Annual conferences convened until occupation or war conditions prohibited. Conferences voted approval of secession, the Georgia Annual Conference acting a month before the state by its commitment. The 1861 Tennessee Annual Conference requested Bishop Joshua Soule to "appoint as many preachers of this conference as he may deem proper to the chaplaincy of our army." Appoint he and the other bishops did. Methodists came to constitute almost half of the Confederate chaplaincy. In fact, of the 1,308 chaplains who served, we know the denominational affiliation of 938. Of these, 46 percent were Methodist.[8] The southern Missionary Society also met and received what would be meager contributions for missions; but it constituted the Southern armies as themselves a mission. The MECS bishops convened concurrently with the Missionary Society and by 1863 recognized Bishop Robert Paine as Methodist superintendent of the army and W. W. Bennett, president of Randolph-Macon, as in charge of publication for the army. Also in 1863, the Missionary Society drafted a nine-point enabling "Army Mission" program. Union occupation of Nashville in 1862 dispersed leadership from MECS headquarters, putting the Missionary Society into its own itineration and shutting down the Methodist Publishing House and the *Nashville Christian Advocate*. Book editor Thomas O. Summers and book agent John B. McFerrin fled. Another editor, Edmund Sehon, stayed, but only to be imprisoned. McFerrin busied himself elsewhere in Tennessee and in Alabama as one of the army missionaries with the troops. Other *Advocates* took up some of the communication and publication slack, all succumbing, however, by war's end.

CHAPLAINS AND ARMY MISSIONARIES

The Methodist army missionaries, as well as local and traveling preachers pastoring (though under arms) along with chaplains, worked the camps, distributing Bibles and tracts, conducting services, holding revivals, organizing army churches, writing letters for soldiers or teaching them to read and write, nursing the wounded, praying with the maimed, burying the dead, and consoling those to be executed.[9] Often chaplains and army missionaries accompanied regiments from their own town or region. The latter were cared for financially by the MECS and sometimes split time between home pulpit and the troops. The former, poorly paid and meagerly provisioned—something of an afterthought within the Confederate army—worked under often indifferent, sometimes hostile, only occasionally supportive commanding officers.[10]

The lack of consistent support from officers—symbols of the elite, the genteel, and planter class—would color ministerial class attitudes thereafter, encouraging greater dependence on and attention to professionals and merchants. Army service also permitted Methodist preachers to attend to their own image and self-image. Functioning as chaplains or missionaries gave preachers opportunity to demonstrate and exhibit the interconnection of piety, patriotism, and manliness and some debated even a further symbolization of male honor—whether chaplains should bear arms.[11]

The revivals and conversions within the Confederate army were points of Southern Methodist pride and self-congratulation long after the war was over, celebrated in the 1877 volume *A Narrative of the Great Revival in the Southern Armies During the Late Civil War Between the States of the Federal Union*.[12] Mission was the Methodist business, so chaplains evangelized from the start. Pastoral care and the distribution of Bibles effectively served that purpose for individual soldiers suffering the tedium of long encampments.[13] Chaplains also conducted revivalistic campaigns, especially in the fall of 1862 and thereafter as the carnage and casualties mounted. Revivals were also stimulated by the initiative of General "Stonewall" Jackson to solicit from denominational leaders and from the chaplains themselves a more regularized ministry—the appointment of more chaplains, their itineration to cover unstaffed regiments, services at headquarters, associations of chaplains for more cooperative endeavor, and better supplies. Jackson's counsel and particularly the formation of chaplains' associations spread throughout the Confederate army. By associating, working together, and offering morning, noon, or tattoo (evening) services, chaplains (Protestants) could sustain significant revival campaigns of a week's duration or even longer. There were reports of two revivals lasting twenty-one days and thirty days, respectively, the first producing 100 and the second 140 conversions. (A Georgia regiment set the record with a revival continuing for four months and five days.)[14] More generalized revivals occurred in the Army of Tennessee and the Army of Northern Virginia. The former produced 321 conversions and 728 church memberships in one month and overall bringing 13 percent of the army into Christian commitment.[15]

Preachers who stayed with or returned to their congregations supported families of the soldiers, visited those hospitalized, and conducted funerals and memorials for those killed—in effect playing chaplains' roles. Confederate chaplaincy exhibited local and conference investment in the war cause. The same can be said for Northern Methodism with respect to the Union.

NORTHERN METHODISTS AND THE WAR

In the North, too, Methodists experienced opposition or indifference to the patriotic banner, especially in the border states. Several conferences had responded vehemently to a stronger Disciplinary statement against slavery in 1860, with Philadelphia demanding repeal, and Baltimore dividing on the question. Kentucky and Missouri, with a small MEC and large MECS population, proved a religious as well as military battleground. In Kentucky, the MECS conference tilted toward the Union cause and some eighteen preachers eventually withdrew and joined the MEC. Southern Methodists in Missouri leaned toward the Confederacy and harassed preachers of the MEC until Northern troops secured the state within the Union and Northern Methodists could return the favor. There, too, members and preachers switched into the MEC.[16] In Ohio, opponents of the war, Southern sympathizers, supporters of the Peace Democrats (specifically the gubernatorial efforts of former congressman Clement L. Vallandigham), and resisters to the abolitionist cause coalesced into a Copperhead church. Calling itself the Christian Union, it survived the war as a holiness denomination, the Churches of Christ in Christian Union.[17]

However, the outbreak of war brought much of the MEC, MPC, The Evangelical Association (EA), and UB churches around to support of the Union, rallied by antislavery editors placed at the helm of the *Christian Advocate* (Edward Thompson) and the *Central Christian Advocate* (Charles Elliott) by the 1860 General Conference. Gilbert Haven (1821–80) assumed the editorship of *Zion's Herald* only after the war. However, throughout the war he contributed to it, to the New York paper, and to the widely read *Independent* columns, essays, and sermons that championed the war as God's cause—indeed as a millennial mandate to cleanse nation (and church) of the sin of slavery (see his appeal in his very first issue in *MEA* 1867*a*). Bishop Matthew Simpson, a friend and confidant of Lincoln and eulogist at his Springfield funeral, spoke frequently and eloquently on behalf of the nation and national unity, against slavery, and for the war as divinely commissioned, and in the effort to raise money for the Union cause (*MEA* 1864*e*). In sermons and exhortations, waving a "battle-torn flag," he evangelized for patriotism, turned revivalism political, elicited camp-meeting fervor, and brought convictions and conversions.[18] During the war, many Northern Methodists swung into a crusade mentality. Conferences passed patriotic resolutions, administered oaths to themselves and their probationers, and called for days of national fasting and prayer. The Philadelphia Conference virtually reversed its actions of the prior year, making loyalty a Disciplinary imperative.

> The class of the second year was called up by the Bishop, and the usual Disciplinary questions asked and answered.
>
> By the direction of the Conference the following question was then proposed to the Class, and answered by each in the affirmative:— "Are you in favor of sustaining the Union, the Government and the Constitution of the United States against the present rebellion?"

And the conference adopted the "Report of Committee on the State of the Country," which denounced the "unjust and wicked rebellion" and prescribed a similar oath of loyalty for all:

> Resolved, 5—That we not only declare our loyalty to the Constitution and Government of these United States in the presence of Almighty God and these witnesses, but that we declare our willingness to swear or affirm the same whenever it shall be required by those who have the rule over us.[19]

Two years later, the Philadelphia Conference instructed "the Presiding Elders . . . not to employ as supplies, any person who is either disloyal or pro-slavery." It reaffirmed previous stands of loyalty, supported the war effort, declared its loyalty to the government and the constitution, urged it as "a religious duty not to speak evil of ministers and magistrates," and denounced slavery as against the law of God and the principles of the Revolution. Philadelphia then endorsed emancipation and rescinded its action of 1861 calling for repeal of the "New Chapter."[20] The 1863 Newark Conference featured a flag-raising service among its six enumerated public services; heard R. B. Yard, chaplain of the First New Jersey Regiment; declared that "[o]ur soldiers are grieved at every evidence of disloyalty at home"; closed one session singing "My Country, 'tis of Thee"; and passed a resolution governing candidates for admission on trial: "<u>Resolved</u>, That the Presiding Elders be requested, when they present the names of candidates for admission on trial, to state whether or not these candidates are loyal to the government of this country." It also affirmed the "Report of the Committee On the State of the Country," with a page and a half of "whereases," the first of which declared "[t]hat unconditional and uncompromising loyalty to the principles and constituted forms of our republican government, is the duty of all Christian people."[21] The 1863 meeting of the National Association of Local Preachers of the Methodist Episcopal Church passed declarations of loyalty "to the Discipline and Government of the Methodist Episcopal Church," to the "Constitution and laws of the United States," and to "the recognized rulers of our nation and the perpetuity of our National Union."[22]

The MEC General Conference of 1864 heard Bishop Thomas A. Morris preach on "the Spirit of Methodism." Beginning ten affirmations with "The Spirit of Methodism is . . . ," Morris characterized Methodism as a church committed to American society, capitalism, progress, and the Union. He enumerated Methodism's spirit as the spirit of truth, the spirit of revival, the spirit of enterprise, the spirit of sacrifice, the spirit of progress, the spirit of improvement, the spirit of loyalty to the civil government, the spirit of patriotism, the spirit of liberty, and the spirit of liberality.[23] Under just such commitments, the MEC General Conference joined other Protestant denominations in petitioning Congress to amend the preamble of the Constitution to affirm God's governance of the country:

> We, the people of the United States, humbly acknowledging Almighty God as the source of all authority and power in civil government, the Lord Jesus Christ as the Ruler among the nations, his revealed will as the supreme law of the land, in order to constitute a Christian government, and in order to form a more perfect union . . .

General Conference's action, in response to its Committee on the State of the Country, issued in series of resolutions calling for recognition of God in the Constitution and amendment of the Constitution to end slavery. It also, belatedly, began the process of revising the General Rules so that holding, buying, or selling slaves would be a bar to church membership.[24]

Northern conferences of the UBC (for instance, Miami [Ohio]), passed similar statements calling for the nation to carry through on the war effort, end the rebellion, and complete the overthrow of slavery with constitutional guarantees of freedom (*MEA* 1864c).[25] Similarly, Methodist Protestantism, having lost much of its Southern and slavery-oriented territory just prior to the Civil War, expressed its support in its 1862 General Conference for the Emancipation Proclamation and its repudiation of disloyalty to the Union cause.[26]

Methodist laity responded to such challenges and volunteered in record numbers, perhaps some 125,000 all told.[27] So did the preachers, both as chaplains and as soldiers. One regiment, the 73rd Illinois, even earned the designation "the preacher regiment" because of the number therein, the result of the mobilizing efforts of one minister, James Jaquess.[28] An Ohio minister, Charles C. McCabe (1836–1906), recruited thousands, his sermons producing the 122nd Ohio Regiment, for which he then served as chaplain. Known as the "singing chaplain," he was captured, incarcerated in the Libby Prison in Richmond, and freed in a prisoner exchange, but not before teaching other prisoners "The Battle Hymn of the Republic." Another recruiter-minister from Ohio, Granville Moody, accepted command of the 74th Ohio Regiment, preaching as well as leading and becoming known as the "gallant fighting preacher."[29]

UNION CHAPLAINS: ORDAINED AND LAY

Methodists constituted the largest chaplain cohort within the Union armies (as with the Confederate side). Of the 2,154 regimental chaplains, 38 percent were Methodist. The next largest confessional contribution came from Presbyterians, at 17 percent.[30] The chaplain role was not much better envisioned on the Union side initially, with both armies being heir to desultory customs and not to statutes concerning chaplains. However, President Lincoln was clearer than Jefferson Davis on their necessity. As war loomed, he wrote seven Washington ministers asking that they serve as military and hospital chaplains. Congress and the War Department followed through with acts and directives establishing the office. Among the requisites were ordination and testimonials of "present good standing with a recommendation for his appointment as an army Chaplain from some authorized ecclesiastical body, or not less than five accredited ministers belonging to said denomination."[31]

Union chaplains worked every bit as ecumenically as their Southern counterparts, partly aided by and partly competing with the U.S. Christian Commission. Founded in 1861 by the YMCA as an evangelistic Protestant counterpart to another relief organization—the U.S. Sanitary Commission— and endorsed by a YMCA-called convention of chaplains, the interdenominational Christian Commission intended to extend the revivalistic triumphs of the 1857–58 "businessmen's awakening" into the Northern armies. With strong lay leadership, aggressive fund-raising, businesslike revivalistic method, and rhetoric of masculine Christianity, the Christian Commission rallied Northern laymen (like Chicagoan and dry goods merchant John V. Farwell [1825–1908]) through its network of YMCA chapters to the cause of evangelizing the troops. Effectively organized, the Christian Commission placed its lay volunteers in the camps and in hospitals and toward the front, each equipped with a handbook of duties and regulations and wearing a badge to signify his commission. Ministering to spirit and body and serving six-week stints, they circulated tracts, Bibles, and Scripture cards; cared for the dying, wounded, and lonely; distributed stamps, envelopes, and stationery; wrote letters for soldiers; and led prayer meetings in "chapel tents" and YMCA rooms. By war's end the Christian Commission had deployed some 5,000 volunteers, handed out 2.5 million publications, preached about 50,000 sermons, and conducted 75,000 prayer meetings. The Christian Commission enjoyed the support of President Lincoln and General Grant, and its ministrations were noted appreciatively by the soldiers in diaries and letters. And with such endorsement, particularly that of Grant, the Commission played an important role in a revival that broke out in the Union armies in late 1863 and continued to 1865—a revival that followed very bloody battles.[32]

The number and percentage of Methodists working within the Christian Commission and who were instrumental in these revivals are hard to calculate. Its volunteers included 458 MEC ministers, and the *Advocates* reported on its work. It enjoyed the backing of key Methodists, among them especially Bishop Edmund S. Janes (1807–76). Elected to the episcopacy in 1844, Janes served as one of the twelve-member Commission and as one of four clergy on it. Along with two other commissioners, he issued the first Circular (November 16, 1861), and, as a member of the executive committee of five, published the Plan of Operations. The Commission sent him to Washington to negotiate with the government on its behalf, and he received from Secretary of War E. M. Stanton a handwritten authorization of access for the Christian Commission "for the performance of their religious and benevolent purposes in the armies of the United States, and in the forts, garrisons, and camps, and military posts." Bishop Matthew Simpson (1811–84) also became part of the Commission, delivering one of the plenary addresses at its 1863 meeting; participating with four other trustees in closing down its work; and summarizing its accomplishments before the House of Representatives.[33] Simpson also figured in another negotiation with Edwin Stanton, namely, that with Bishop E. R. Ames, which empowered the MEC to take over confiscated MECS churches. Charles McCabe, after release from prison, labored for the Commission in fund-raising, established a personal goal of $250,000, and perfected patterns of promotion that would later transform denominational practice. However, it was Methodist laity, along with laity from other Protestant denominations in the Christian Commission, who led the revivals in the Northern armies, converting between 100,000 and 200,000 men. Impressive revivals—a veritable "pentecostal season"—broke out in 1864 and continued till war's end in the Union armies in Virginia and Tennessee and within the army marching south with Sherman. Sherman's troops took Charleston "singing Methodist hymns."[34]

ORGANIZATION AND SPECIALIZATION

The two world wars would again create demand and opportunity for chaplains in great numbers. The MPC, MECS, and MEC each created commissions during World War I to elicit and oversee the church's ministry to the armed forces. Some 325 Methodists served as chaplains. The newly reunited Methodism created a Commission on Chaplains in 1942. By 1944 it had deployed 1,300 chaplains. In 1948, the Methodist Church regularized the Commission on Chaplains as an agency with oversight responsibilities for hospital, military, prison, and reformatory chaplaincies.

Chaplaincies in the health and welfare area and in higher education (now a huge cohort) swelled over the course of the twentieth century. They did so as these great nineteenth-century institutional investments on the part of the church—homes, hospitals, colleges, and universities—increasingly and for reasons of law and efficiency turned for staff and leadership to professionals. No longer headed by a Methodist preacher, who could administer with some pastoral sensitivity, these institutions needed ministers with training and skills suited for those particular settings. Seminaries, universities, and the health care industry generated new pastoral specializations and specialized training programs. One important such specialization has been clinical pastoral education (CPE), the route into health care ministries for many seminarians.

In turn, the church has responded to new institutional and ministry needs with its own training programs, credentialing processes, ministerial offices, and supervisory organization. The turn of the twentieth century saw incredible energy devoted to the deaconess program, which equipped women for ministries of care, healing, intervention, and advocacy, particularly for urban settings. In the late twentieth century some diaconal ministries and the new, ordained deacons took on chaplaincy or chaplaincy-type roles. However, many of the settings call for ministries of Word and Sacrament and the church has continued to invest elders with these extension responsibilities. And so the church now entrusts to the Division of Ordained Ministry of the General Board of Higher Education and Ministry the responsibility of overseeing candidacies, setting and maintaining educational and training standards, and endorsing and supporting chaplaincies for "health-care settings, children's homes, retirement homes, prisons, workplaces, counseling centers, and the military."[35] Despite common rubrics, these several chaplaincies seem to function as fairly discrete professions, each with its own way of congregating and resourcing itself. And each of the chaplain cohorts, like much of extension ministry, seems marginal to conference life—a distancing symbolized if not reinforced by the credentialing, accountability, and resourcing relation to the General Board of Higher Education and Ministry.

AFTERWORD

Earlier Methodism was clear that chaplaincy belonged to its ministry, that Methodists recognized one vocation—that of preacher—and that chaplains and regular itinerants were called to the one ministry. Methodism affirmed this understanding by linking the ministry to appointment by the bishop. It did so as well by listing together those who, though appointed and, in some cases, elected by General Conference, needed to be exempted from the two-year limit because of the tenure needed for the effective fulfillment of their duties:

> [The] presiding elders, the general editor, the general book steward and his assistant, the editor and assistant editor of the Christian Advocate and Journal, the editor of the Sunday school books, the corresponding secretaries, editors and agents at Cincinnati, the supernumerary, superannuated and worn-out preachers, missionaries among the Indians, missionaries to our people of colour and on foreign stations, chaplains to state prison and military posts . . .[36]

Paul's counsel to leaders among the Ephesians and the wonderful hymn version by Charles Wesley apply in a fitting way to chaplains. Many put on special garb that arm them "with all the mind / That was in Christ," our Head, and know on a daily basis that the Christian life must be something of a battle against earthly and cosmic powers of darkness and evil. Chaplains do extend the ministry of the church into domains where killing reigns (the military); where suffering and pain prevail (hospitals); and where inquiry, research, and teaching sometimes undercut the conviction of believers (education). Yet witness for the faith on these barriers belongs to the entire ministry. And the counsel of Paul and Wesley applies to the whole body of Christ and its several ministries—lay, licensed, commissioned, consecrated, ordained, full-time, and part-time: All need "the helmet of salvation, and the sword of the Spirit, which is the word of God" (Eph. 6:17). All need to be "Strong in the Lord of hosts, / And in his mighty power," and we know that everyone who "in the strength of Jesus trusts / Is more than conqueror."

4

Connecting: An Extension Task[1]

Luke 1:46-55

[46]And Mary said,
  "My soul magnifies the Lord,
    [47]and my spirit rejoices in God my Savior,
[48]for he has looked with favor on the lowliness of his servant.
    Surely, from now on all generations will call me blessed;
[49]for the Mighty One has done great things for me,
    and holy is his name.
[50]His mercy is for those who fear him
    from generation to generation.
[51]He has shown strength with his arm;
    he has scattered the proud in the
        thoughts of their hearts.
[52]He has brought down the powerful from their thrones,
    and lifted up the lowly;
[53]he has filled the hungry with good things,
    and sent the rich away empty.
[54]He has helped his servant Israel,
    in remembrance of his mercy,
[55]according to the promise he made to our ancestors,
    to Abraham and to his descendants forever."

—⁓—

1   All glory to God in the sky,[2]
        And peace upon earth be restored!
     O Jesus exalted on high,
        Appear our omnipotent Lord!
     Who meanly in Bethlehem born,
        Didst stoop to redeem a lost race,
     Once more to thy creatures return,
        And reign in thy kingdom of grace.

2   When thou in our flesh didst appear,
        All nature acknowledged thy birth;
     Arose the acceptable year,
        And heaven was opened on earth.
     Receiving its Lord from above,
        The world was united to bless
     The giver of concord and love,
        The Prince and the author of peace.

3   O wouldst thou again be made known!
        Again in thy Spirit descend;
     And set up in each of thine own
        A kingdom that never shall end.
     Thou only art able to bless,
        And make the glad nations obey,
     And bid the dire enmity cease,
        And bow the whole world to thy sway.

4   Come then to thy servants again,
        Who long thy appearing to know;
     Thy quiet and peaceable reign
        In mercy establish below;
     All sorrow before thee shall fly,
        And anger and hatred be o'er;
     And envy and malice shall die,
        And discord afflict us no more.

5 No horrid alarum of war
    Shall break our eternal repose,
No sound of the trumpet is there,
    Where Jesus's Spirit o'erflows:
Appeased by the charms of thy grace
    We all shall in amity join,
And kindly each other embrace,
    And love with a passion like thine.

—⟨⟨⟩⟩—

Extension, special, or ABLC ("appointments beyond the local church") ministries, I have suggested, institutionalized roles that Wesley had played and offices that he had exercised for the preachers and people connected to him, the people called Methodist. True to form, American Methodists established versions of these functions—publishers, missionaries, fund-raisers (colporteurs) for colleges and secondary schools, and corresponding (general) secretaries of Methodist and interdenominational missionary, Bible, tract, and Sunday school societies; faculty in Methodist schools, and chaplains (prison or army)—as connectional offices, defining them as such in the *Discipline* and endeavoring to provide oversight appropriate to their connectional nature.

These offices emerged neither at once nor simultaneously. This chapter charts the emergence of extension ministries and attempts to discern what roles they played in connecting Methodism. I suggest (with perhaps just a little exaggeration) that extension ministries actually functioned to connect and hold together a Methodism otherwise exploding centrifugally—a Methodism whose highest body sat only briefly every four years and whose key leaders, the bishops, found reasons to go their separate ways. To begin, a few words about Methodist connectionalism.[3]

The Connectional Church in American Society

Commentators on the American scene sometimes speak of churches as connectional in nature. With that term they differentiate denominations with strong corporate, centralized, or hierarchical authority systems from those with systems that are self-consciously or operationally congregational, independent, or free-church.[4] While lacking precision the word handily marks off episcopal and presbyterial from congregational polities. So the Roman Catholic, Orthodox, Lutheran, Episcopal, and Presbyterian churches are connectional, while Baptist, Congregational (UCC), Christian, and Mennonite churches are not. Connectional communions, if Protestant, by and large derive from the Magisterial Reformation and often have enjoyed privileged status as state or established churches. So Lutheran churches were established in Germany and Scandinavia, the Reformed or Presbyterian churches in Scotland and Switzerland, and Anglican churches in England. By contrast, many, though not all, of the non-connectional churches have roots or affinities with the Radical Reformation and a free-church ecclesiology.[5]

Anabaptist and Baptist churches illustrate that trajectory. The latter fit comfortably within American social and legal patterns, where voluntarism, separation of church and state, localism, free enterprise, and individualism hold sway. Connectional churches, by contrast, have had episodic clashes with the courts or with popular opinion, both of which presume that churches are local bodies "owned" by trustees. To a public, and even a membership, that "knows" religion to be voluntary, connectional churches have had to explain themselves. "What do you mean we don't own this church?" inquire parishioners. And trustees add: "We paid every dime to build it and pay every dollar now to maintain it." The burden of explaining connectional authority and connectional title to property has been borne most heavily by the Roman Catholics; but virtually all connectional churches can recall some moment of conflict around connectionalism.[6] Many Methodists express surprise when informed of the "trust clause" and conference title to their church. This angularity of connectionalism with respect to American values and practice puts it forth as a term for distinction.

METHODIST CONNECTIONALISM

United Methodism and many other American Methodist communions would certainly place themselves among the connectional churches. Our connectionalism, most Methodists would know, does not derive, in the first instance, from the Magisterial Reformation or the privileged status as a state church. While United Methodism and other episcopal Methodisms do owe much to Anglicanism, it was John and Charles Wesley (preeminently John) who defined our connectionalism.[7] The term has a special meaning for Methodists, a meaning I mention here and return to in a later chapter.

The connectionalism derived from Wesley was decidedly enriched by elements of Anglican ecclesiology and practice and by American organizational experience, especially in its recent corporate forms. For some interpreters, it is these later accretions, such as apportionments and corporate bureaucratic boards and agencies that spend the apportionments, that most define connectionalism. And when Methodists reshape the church through mergers, these later accretions tend to preoccupy the architects of the new orders.

Nothing symbolizes centralized authority better than taxes; and, for Methodists, apportionments vividly convey certain notions of connection and connectionalism. In the minds of most Methodists—members and officers—apportionments represent the claim of centralized authority—a claim that comes as an "obligatory" budgetary asking. To the typical United Methodist, connectionalism means taxation, begrudged even for the pension and salary portions that she understands. Connectionalism has always had its fiscal dimension. Indeed, one might argue that connectionalism had its foundation in the collection of 1742 that inaugurated the class system. Since then, being in connection with Mr. Wesley had its price. Certainly, early American Methodism depended entirely on the collections brought to quarterly conference, the quarterage shared equally among itinerants, presiding elders, and bishops. Nor is this the first generation of Methodists who have chafed under collections that supported far-off ministries.

However, though impossible and unthinkable without its fiscal dimension, connectionalism has always meant more than sharing a financial burden.

Indeed, it has been bearable as a financial burden because it was embraced and celebrated for its *multiple* values. Recalling these multiple values helps United Methodists understand why we speak of ourselves as a connectional church and why we simply must think of more than apportionments when we think "connection."

The remainder of this chapter, and the chapters to follow, explore these multiple values. I begin by exploring Methodism as a changing covenant, noting the different forms or styles of connectionalism that have emerged over the history of American Methodism. In an earlier day, Methodists would have noted these creations as providentially given and would have unabashedly celebrated God's hand in their machinery. Here we would do well to be reminded of God's work through the ages, articulated in the Magnificat and the Wesley hymn at the beginning of this chapter—of God's promise to help God's servant Israel from generation to generation and of the hope for that prefigured peaceable reign. For those who believe grace to be responsible, the corporate response to God's initiative can well have connectional shape.

CONNECTIONALISM: A PRACTICAL DIVINITY AND A CHANGING COVENANT

At its best, then, Methodist connectionalism has been more than a form of corporatism, a polity, or a classificatory term. Connectionalism has been a Wesleyan precept, an ecclesial vision, a missional principle, a covenantal commitment, an ethic of equity and proportionality, a tactical stratagem, an elastic and evolving standard, and a theology in praxis. Only if these richer meanings are understood can one appreciate why we give them fiscal expression. We can grasp that richness best if we remind ourselves how significantly we have changed the connection—our connective tissue, our way of connecting—over time. And in each transition we see yet another extension ministry emerge, the connective form for a new day.

In living their theology, Methodists indeed gave connectionalism different shape in different periods. They held themselves together, undertook their mission, defined their identity, communicated with one another, and structured their governance in styles appropriate for the day. Each style had its own grammar and rules touching form, substance, procedure, and structure. And each produced a distinctive connectional leadership style. Several of these leadership roles now belong to the extension category. The others arguably could as well.

Seven different connectional styles seem distinct enough to warrant mention and brief characterization. I term these styles Wesleyan (episcopal), popular, voluntary, corporate, federal, professional, and post-corporate. I have arrayed them here in roughly chronological order, though the first two emerged at virtually the same time. The fifth, the federal, has been in the process of development over the whole of our history, and several others have also evolved over long periods of time. Further, the several connectional stratagems and their corresponding leadership pattern all live on. One style does not disappear after its period of dominance but instead remains to find altered place in the successive connectional periods. These seven styles represent continuing options for Methodist self-understanding, definition of mission, and connectional shaping. They function as historical generalizations, as a typology, as models.

Oral/Aural Connection

How, over the course of its history, did American Methodism connect itself? Of what did its connectionalism consist? How did it structure and display its theology?[8] In its first decades, American Methodism implemented and depended upon the connectional, missional, and Disciplinary provisions that Wesley had developed—evangelistic and expansive; that is, extension in style if there ever were such. It enriched and decorated these provisions after 1784 with the episcopal features taken over from Anglicanism.[9] Conferences, itinerating general superintendents, a national itinerant ministry, and classes for the Methodist people connected the dynamic young movement and gave voice to Methodism's Arminian and grace-laden word. Wesleyan connectionalism had a distinctive character, look, *and* voice. Unlike the prevailing denominational systems (confined within boundaries of parish, ethnicity, or language), Methodism knew no boundaries, indeed aspiring from the start to reform the continent. Methodists preached and testified wherever they could to whomever would listen, voicing the invitation to belong. Connection had a preeminently *oral/aural* character (a style every bit as characteristic of the United Brethren and Evangelical movements as of the Methodist Episcopal). Preaching mediated a Wesleyan reading of Scripture; hymns instilled our doctrines; class meetings translated promise into practice; and love feasts expressed the joy that young and old, rich and poor, white and black, English and German had *heard* and *experienced*. Methodist connectionalism *voiced* itself and measured its effectiveness by the quality, intensity, and volume of its utterance. Did one preach with "liberty"? elicit tears? demand or produce shouts and cries? Virtually any journal or diary of this period attests and assesses this voiced connectionalism. For instance, Jesse Lee noted for late 1783 and for 1784:

> [Dec.] Saturday 31st, I preached at Mr. Spain's with great liberty to a good congregation, and the Spirit of the Lord came upon us, and we were bathed in tears—I wept—and so loud were the people's cries, that I could scarcely be heard, though I spoke very loud. I met the class—most of the members expressed a great desire for holiness of heart and life, and said they were determined to seek for perfect love.
>
> Sunday 1st of February, I preached at Coleman's with life and liberty, to a weeping congregation. When I met the class, we were highly favoured of the Lord, with a comfortable sense of his love shed abroad in our hearts; the brethren wept, and praise God together. . . .
>
> Saturday 14th.—We held our quarterly meeting for Amerlia Circuit, at old father Patrick's—we had a good meeting for the first day. On Sunday morning we had a happy love feast; at which time I wept much, and prayed earnestly that the Lord would take every evil temper and every wrong desire out of my heart, and fill my soul with perfect love. I felt the pain of parting with my friends in that circuit . . .[10]

Preaching, singing, testifying—early Methodists voiced their love for one another and so quite literally heard themselves together. And in connecting themselves to one another and to their mission, they heeded the variety of rubrics, practices, and offices that Wesley had given them. Connectionalism had a specifically Wesleyan grammar and vocabulary. And the rules were those taken over from Wesley and adjusted to the American scene and episcopal governance in what Americans called a *Discipline*. In its thirty pages[11] or so, Methodists found guidance for spreading scriptural holiness. So Methodism connected itself through an itinerant general superintendent (and specifically Asbury), annual and general conferences, and a nationally itinerant traveling ministry (itinerants and presiding elders whom Asbury appointed across conference lines and on a national basis, reinforcing his own itinerant general superintendency with an itinerant general ministry). The ministry, the episcopacy, and the conferences constituted a particularly important and underappreciated connective voice.

Methodism hung together in hearing a common Arminian gospel. And it did so depending upon a very distinctive leadership cadre and style of leading—itinerant general superintendency and appointed/appointive itinerancy. Missionary, evangelistic, expansive—*extension* ministry if there ever were such—these forms are not now so categorized. Indeed, these bedrock, Wesleyan, Disciplinary understandings of leadership continue to this day as normative United Methodist ministerial forms. Coincidentally, as we have noted, by a great inversion, superintendency looks diocesan rather than itinerant and general, and itinerancy looks very much like the Anglicanism Mr. Wesley sought to reform.

Connected by Event

A second style of connectionalism also derives from the earliest phases of Methodism and featured the leadership of the presiding elder (district superintendent). It represented a further "Americanization" of the Wesleyan *extension* or missionary style and is so intertwined with the first as to be infrequently distinguished. William Everett and Thomas Frank isolate and name it, describing it as popular public assembly.[12] This designation contextualizes early Methodist gatherings—crowds taken outside for preaching, the quarterly meeting and love feast, the camp meeting, the assemblages around conference—in the long tradition of Christian (and secular) popular gatherings. I prefer a more regional understanding of this leadership style, namely, as the religious counterpart to the event-based community of the upper South and lower-middle states.[13] Like elections, musters, dances, and horse races, Methodist community was an event, defined less by space or place than by time, by something that happened. Connectionalism *occurred*—*by appointment*. It was *event*.

Its event character was well captured by the admonition, "Don't disappointment an appointment!" Of the events constitutive of and connectional for Methodism, the most important and expressive was the quarterly meeting over which the presiding elder (when that office appeared) "presided." In it the ecclesial dimensions of conference, outlined above, came alive most fully. One key to the quarterly conference's connective role came from an early change in design and length, an important adaptation of the Wesleyan institution. In 1780 the American conference recommended that quarterly meetings be a two-day affair and a weekend event, whenever possible.[14] From that point on the quarterly meeting quite literally brought the connection together, as this very early account indicates:

> I went next morning to brother Hobb's. Next day, was our quarterly-meeting, and a great many people came out; here I met brother Whatcoat and brother Morrell; one of them preached, and the other exhorted. Next day, brother Whatcoat opened the love-feast; and after the bread and water were handed round, divers young converts spoke very feelingly of the goodness of God, and his dealings with their souls: we had a precious time. There was a large congregation, and one of our brethren preached, and the other gave an exhortation: we had a solemn, and I trust, a profitable time to many souls.[15]

Bishop Thomas Coke provides a particularly interesting perspective because his view indicates from the highest possible British Methodist authority the novelty of the American quarterly meeting.

> Their Quarterly-meetings on this Continent are much attended to. The Brethren for twenty miles round, and sometimes for thirty or forty, meet together. The meeting always lasts two days. All the Travelling Preachers in

the Circuit are present, and they with perhaps a local Preacher or two, give the people a sermon one after another, besides the Love-feast, and (now) the Sacraments. On Saturday 9, I set off with the friends to Brother *Martin's*, in whose barn I preached that day. The next day I administered the Sacrament to a large company, and preached, and after me the two Travelling Preachers. We had now been six hours and a half engaged in duty, and I had published myself to preach in the neighbourhood for the three following days, so they deferred the second Love-Feast till Wednesday.[16]

The early *Disciplines* specified a short set of duties for the presiding elder, among them presiding at quarterly meetings:

Quest. 2. What are the duties of a presiding elder?
Answ. 1. To travel through his appointed district.
2. In the absence of a bishop, to take charge of all the elders, deacons, travelling and local preachers, and exhorters in his district.
3. To change, receive, or suspend preachers in his district during the intervals of the conferences, and in the absence of the bishop.
4. In the absence of a bishop, to preside in the conference.
5. To be present, as far as practicable, at all the quarterly meetings: . . .

When bishops Francis Asbury and Thomas Coke glossed this section of the *Discipline*, they concluded by crediting the presiding elders, to a significant extent, with the missionary or evangelistic successes of the young movement.

In the year 1784, when the presiding eldership did, *in fact*, though not in *name*, commence, there were about 14000 in society on this continent; and now the numbers amount to upwards of 56000: so that the society is, at present, four times as large as it was twelve or thirteen years ago. We do not believe that the office now under consideration was the *principal cause* of this great revival, but the Spirit and grace of God, and the consequent zeal of the preachers in general. Yet we have no doubt, but the full organization of our body, and giving to the whole a complete and effective executive government, of which the presiding eldership makes a very capital branch, has, under God, been a grand means of preserving the peace and union of our connection and the purity of our ministry, and, therefore, *in its consequences*, has been a *chief instrument*, under the grace of God, of this great revival.[17]

The event-based character of Methodist connectionalism displayed itself most extravagantly in the institution that housed warm-weather quarterly meetings, namely, the camp meeting. As events, camp meetings oriented the Methodist connection toward its mission, namely, to redeem individuals and society. This engagement with the world and the worldly, often rough-and-tumble, gave them their storied character. If they indeed housed a quarterly meeting, which was the early standard, then the presiding elder had the responsibility of overseeing the event.

One gets a sense of the office of presiding elder and of the rough-and-tumble missional and strategic character of the office, particularly as it led the evangelistic expansion of the church into frontier areas, in the autobiographical tall tales of Peter Cartwright, notably in his *Autobiography of Peter Cartwright, the Backwoods Preacher* (1856) and *Fifty Years as a Presiding Elder* (1871).[18] Cartwright regales the reader with tale after tale about camp meetings without explaining why he had to be present and why he spent virtually his entire summer in camp—that he was a presiding elder. The most thorough study of the exercise of the office up through Cartwright's period, that by Fred Price, makes the case for its strategic nature. His theme—*The Role of the Presiding Elder in the Growth of the Methodist Episcopal Church*—carried throughout the volume and in the title, is that the presiding eldership was missional in character and the key to Methodism's explosive growth. It was the missional operational agency of the church and its chief evangelistic office.[19]

Recollections make clear the importance of the quarterly meeting over which the presiding elder presided:

> The old quarterly meeting conferences and love-feasts! what was more characteristic of practical Methodism than they? The horses and carriages, and groups of men, women, and children plodding the highways on foot, for twenty miles or more, as on a holy pilgrimage; the assemblage of preachers, traveling and local, from all the neighboring appointments; the two days of preaching and exhorting, praying and praising; the powerful convictions, and more powerful conversions; and especially the Sunday morning love-feast, with its stirring testimonies and kindling songs; its tears and shout-

ings—how precious their reminiscences! Alas, for the changes which are coming over us![20]

Nowadays, the *Discipline* considers the district superintendent, along with other cabinet appointments, as "in ministry settings beyond the local United Methodist church in the witness and service of Christ's love and justice" and as "Appointments Extending the Ministry of The United Methodist Church."[21] That seems appropriate given the original and vital nature of the office and its evangelistic/missional charge. However, no office competes with its centrality to conference life and its place within the appointment structure. To that extent the office of district superintendent (and other cabinet staff) seems strangely grouped with other ministries gathered into the extension category.

Connection by Press and Voluntary Society

What would connect Methodism—link Methodists to one another, voice their common affirmations, and give expression to their mission—as event (camp meetings) and orality (the shout) waned? Itineration increasingly occurred within conferences. Multiple bishops lacked the cohesive and connective power that had been Asbury's, and the bishops soon began itinerating by region. General Conferences, as we will note below, became, especially after the 1808 provisions for constitutional status and delegation, the important legislative connection.[22] But General Conference met only every four years. Who or what would connect, day-to-day, week-to-week, as had Asbury and his lieutenants? How would Methodism hear a common Word?

The printed page gradually assumed the connecting, mediating, grace-delivering, missional role previously carried by the spoken word; and the *voluntary association* became the vehicle for much of what had been provided through the large popular event. We noted in chapter 1 the early emergence of a special status for book agents (along with missionaries and educators) and the church's struggle to envision and care connectionally for such important extension roles. Their capacity to serve as *the* connectors in an expanding Methodism emerged gradually. Under the leadership of Joshua Soule, book agent/editor (1816–20), and particularly his successor, Nathan Bangs, the Book Concern became the most innovative and connecting force in Methodist life (a role clearly increasing in importance during the preceding decade). The publishing enterprise developed in a number of directions but none more important than the establishment of media for regular communication. *The Methodist Magazine* (1818) and the *Christian Advocate* (1826) provided the church with a clear voice that could convey across the connection complicated and complex ideas in coherent fashion and in a uniform message despite itinerants' varying efforts in and enthusiasm for the published wares. The magazine for clergy, and, more important, the weekly paper for the whole church, focused the entire church's efforts for nurture and outreach. (The United Brethren published the *Zion's Advocate* from 1829 to 1831 and followed with *The Religious Telescope*, a bi-weekly, English-language paper that lasted until union in 1946. The Evangelical Association launched its journal, *Der Christliche Botschafter*, in 1836. Initially a monthly publication, it lasted until the union as a German paper but gradually was upstaged by the English paper *Evangelical Messenger*, begun in 1848.) Connection came through paper, tract, hymnbook, *Discipline*, and Bible. Every itinerant peddled for the Book Concern. Regional *Advocates*, their editors also elected by General Conference, came eventually to nuance Methodism's written word for our many audiences. Through them, Methodism transmitted its "word" to its many publics, allowing Methodists to hear one another across the entire connection.

Also keeping Methodists, United Brethren, and Evangelicals on the same page were the new voluntary societies that focused the common faith toward concerted witness. The Missionary Society of the Methodist Episcopal Church was formed in 1819/20 and the Sunday School Union in 1827 (counterpart organizations for the Evangelicals and United Brethren formed in 1838 and 1841 [missions] and roughly 1820 and 1835 [Sunday schools]). These two programmatic associations came to have great connective power across the Methodist peoples, drawing them into local and conference associations and these associations into action on behalf of the cause. They prospered (as did voluntary movements across American Protestantism) because the church threw its shoulder behind this reorganization and because the new media from the book agency reinforced the organizational efforts. Popular literature, particularly for Sunday schools, made the program of the church available to every Methodist community.

Nathan Bangs saw the importance of these new institutions within the larger Methodist connectional system. After commenting on classes, stewards, exhorters, local preachers, itinerants, conferences, and bishops, he noted:

> In addition to this regular work, in which we behold a beautiful gradation of office and order, from the lowest to the highest, there is the book establishment, which has grown up with the growth of the church, and from which are issued a great variety of books on all branches of theological knowledge, suited to ministers of the gospel, including such as are suited to youth and children, as well as those for Sabbath schools, and a great number of tracts for gratuitous distribution by tract societies, Bibles and Testaments of various sizes, a quarterly review, and weekly religious papers. This establishment is conducted by a suitable number of agents and editors, who are elected by the General Conference, to which body they are responsible for their official conduct, and, in the interval of the General, the New York Annual Conference exercises a supervision of this estimable and highly useful establishment.
>
> In the last place, we may mention the Missionary Society of the Methodist Episcopal Church, which was organized in 1819, and has since spread itself, by means of auxiliary and branch societies, all over the United States and Territories, and, by means of its missionaries, has extended its operations among the aboriginal tribes of our wildernesses, among the descendants of Africa in the south, the new and poorer white settlements of our country, and also has sent its living heralds to Africa, to South America, and to the Oregon Territory. May its boundaries continually enlarge![23]

Both Sunday school and missions channeled Methodist lay imagination and energies into the building of great networks of loosely related societies, male and female, zealously committed to evangelization of youth and the "heathen." Methodists still connected with oral testimony and the written word but increasingly channeled their witness through societies with a missional or programmatic purpose. They did so by joining, and joining with others. The program of the church ran with *voluntary* societies.

Elders in full connection were elected to head these appointments beyond the local church—the Methodist publishing enterprise, the *Advocates*, and the missionary, Sunday school, and tract societies. Their functions and operations linked them to the entire connection and they enjoyed prominent status in General Conferences and, of course, in the annual meetings of their own organization. They enjoyed similar high visibility across the church; appeared personally in annual conferences, at camp meetings, and in other gatherings to promote their respective cause; and consistently received the highest accolade from their own conference, namely, election and reelection to General Conference. The church as a whole affirmed their connectional importance by routinely electing them to the episcopacy. Could extension ministry be given greater prominence? It could be and it was.

Programmed and Corporate Connection

By the 1870s, the church's "extension" ministries, the voluntary societies— then including, for the MEC, the Missionary Society, the Church Extension Society, the Board of Education, the Sunday-School Union and the Tract Society, as well as the more loosely related Freedmen's Aid Society and Book Concern, not to mention temperance organizations, preachers' aid societies, and various others—had become too successful, General Conferences thought, to be allowed to run themselves, to compete with one another, and to remain self-governing. And so in 1872 and 1874, the MEC and MECS took action to make the boards elective and thereby accountable to General Conference, thus turning voluntary societies into national, corporate, denominational boards. A. J. Kynett explained the magnitude of the change in relation to his own agency four years later, noting that previously:

> [a]lthough organized by order of the General Conference, the corporate body was, by the terms of its Constitution and Charter, a "Society" composed of such members and friends of the Church as might contribute to its funds the sum of one dollar per annum, or twenty dollars at one time. These

had the legal right to elect its managers; but only such as could be present at the annual meetings in Philadelphia could share in the exercise of this right. It was, therefore, clearly beyond the reach of the Church government, and equally beyond the reach of all contributors to its funds, except only a portion of those who resided in the city of Philadelphia.[24]

The change effected in 1872 was structural and legal, as indicated in the enabling report:

> The special Committee "appointed to consider and report concerning the relations of our various benevolent societies to the authorities of the Church, and whether any action is necessary, and if so what, to place them under the full control of the General Conference," has considered the subject stated...
>
> With respect to the Missionary Society incorporated by the New York Legislature, it noted "To place this corporation under the control of the General Conference, it will be proper to procure an act of the Legislature to amend the charter so as to provide that the Board of Managers shall be elected by the General Conference."[25]

Connectionalism (and extension ministry) had, at last, a denominational-structural expression, a corporate structure. Agencies proved remarkable connectional delivery systems, serving missional, identity-providing, communicative, and governance functions. These roles and their operation on a national level my colleagues Everett and Frank detail with some care.[26] The corporate structure imprinted itself as well on conference and local levels, each of which structured itself to mimic the national organizational pattern and thereby facilitate programmatic and communication connection. Local Methodists, conference committees, and national boards embraced corporate structure for what it facilitated: effective programs. And programs expressed Methodist ideals and ideas in missions, education, witness, and reform. Those engaged and leading in these several areas enjoyed the energetic and active support of the Methodist folk. Their national heads—the editors and general board secretaries—sustained the high profile of their predecessors. James Buckley (1836–1920), elected editor of the national (New York) *Christian Advocate* after pastoring in several conferences, dominated twelve General Conferences

(1872–1916). As long-time editor (1880–1912), Buckley exercised enormous power, swaying Methodist opinion for good and ill (heading the opposition to women's inclusion in conference affairs).[27] Counterparts in the MECS, the MPC, the UB Church, and the EA enjoyed similar prominence and clout.

Until 1939 or so, the *Advocates* and boards and agencies were surrounded with other bodies, also active on a churchwide level, that bound the connection together and worked programmatically. These included, of course, the college or board of bishops and General Conference but also other national organizations (women's, youth, reform, temperance, etc.), clergy magazines, the seminaries (particularly Boston in the North and Vanderbilt in the South), and the publishing houses. Two twentieth-century developments, however, functioned to undercut the once-close association of the leadership in local and conference affairs. One of these erosive developments functioned so gradually and pervasively in denominational and American life as to go largely undetected. The other can be dated.

Federal-Style Connection

Incidentally, the union of 1939, in the endeavor to create one national Methodist Church out of the separate denominations (MEC, MECS, MPC), tore much of the connectional fabric; or, to put it more judiciously, created a new, federal-style, separation-of-powers connectionalism. Over time, the changes would greatly empower the most prominent extension ministries—those exercised through the general boards—but in so doing would isolate and insulate them from the Methodist people and from the day-to-day life of annual conferences. If significant dates could be put on the marginalization of extension ministries, 1939 would be one of them.

Constitutionally, the 1939 union built "distance" into Methodism. It did so most dramatically with the race-segregated jurisdictions. By placing black membership from the MEC and the MPC into one jurisdiction—the Central Jurisdiction—the new church distanced southern white Methodists from their black co-religionist neighbors. Segregated jurisdictions, a "federal" signature of the 1939 union, functioned thereafter as electoral colleges. Into them the church dropped the key power to elect bishops. Jurisdictions also took over from General Conference the authority gained in 1872/74—that of selecting the directors or members of the general boards. Another federal aspect of 1939 (like jurisdictions, a condition of MECS participation) was the creation of the Judicial Council, brought into being so General Conference could not rule on the constitutionality of its own acts (in effect, the MEC plan); nor were the bishops collectively so authorized (the MECS pattern). A council of bishops gave Methodism something of a look of an upper house or chamber (Senate, House of Bishops) though it would take almost half a century for the bishops to find ways of making that much more than their conference, their fraternity. Although bishops enjoyed that connectional gathering and continued to be elected to preside over boards, by their election and appointment they became provincial, indeed, increasingly diocesan, not general superintendents.[28]

The actions of 1939 consolidated within Methodist *governance* patterns and practices that had long characterized American politics, in particular:

- separating powers and distinguishing between legislative, executive, and judicial functions;
- providing for judicial review;
- delimiting national authority and reserving powers and prerogatives to regional bodies (jurisdiction and conference);
- empowering jurisdictions as electoral colleges;
- construing Methodist conference structures at all levels as representative bodies and therefore as inclusive of laity as well as clergy in accord with principles of equity and proportionality.

One further change (apparently initiated at General Conference and not part of the reunification package) empowered the boards to elect their own professional staff. When combined with the other 1939 developments, this change consolidated boards into even more significant bureaucracies. The net effect of these changes was to leave the agencies as *the* connecting power nationally *and* to undo the accountability that 1872 had achieved. In the union of 1939, rather than that of 1968, lies many of the concerns that today trouble critics of agencies (and of extension ministries more generally).

A few delegates foresaw the problems in conferring on the national boards (themselves increased to what had once been "conference" size) the power of determining their own leadership.[29] According to its defenders, the proposal honored professionalism—election of an agency's staff by its own board. This prerogative, one proponent explained, accorded with "the usual practice when you are seeking experts, as these boards will require, to perform an expert job." Would the nearly 800 members of the new General Conference have the competence, leisure, and judgment to choose as wisely? Speaking for the committee, Paul Quillian thought not. He raised the specter of the great mass of General Conference acting mob-like in selection and of the ephemeral character of General Conferences. He then contrasted this scenario with the informed and careful selection possible in board election: "If you are a member of a general board at the present ask yourself this question: Would you desire to serve during the coming four years with your administrative officers chosen carefully by your General Board or chosen by the General Conference who did not understand your particular problems?"[30] A few thought that staff professionalism sacrificed important denominational values. J. M. M. Gray (Detroit Annual Conference) insisted:

> [I]n some fashion we must combat effectively the disintegrating influence of Jurisdictional lines upon our general connectional influence. And when we elect all our secretaries by boards and elect all our boards by Jurisdictions we have flung away the last of the great influences that have bound us together as a connection.
>
> I am in favor of the election of the Secretary by the General Conference.

Agreeing, the conservative leader from New Jersey and then editor of the *Christian Advocate*, Harold Paul Sloan, spoke against the tendency to "ensmall" the church and of the divisive potential of elections by the boards of their staff.

> 1) I feel there is grave danger of breaking our great American Methodism up into a lot of small groups, each Board will be a group, each Jurisdiction will be a group, and the large interests of the Church instead of coming into focus in the great United General Conference, will never come to focus at all, but will be in expression in these small groups.

2) [T]he responsibility in most instances with these executive leaders is a responsibility in which they can commend themselves to the Church as a whole. A man who has not made an impression upon the Church as a whole as an effective leader for a Board ought not to be elected to that place.

3) [W]e masses do elect the President of the United States . . . we ought to be able to pick out a man big enough to run a Methodist board. . . . [T]he Methodist Church, if it moves from election in its General Conference back to election in its board, is going in exactly the opposite direction from that in which political life in America is going.

4) [Y]ou will open the door to the influence of smaller values upon the creating of these great offices.[31]

Sloan got it right. With General Conference meeting every four years and only briefly, and with key decision making relegated to jurisdictions and bishops-turned-diocesan, the church found the general boards to be the effective connectional structures in this new federal order. And if not exactly "ensmalled," the boards and their leadership found themselves increasingly distanced from local and conference life. That gulf symbolized and reinforced the marginalization of the several ministries that shared the extension status, a marginalization fostered by a long-term societal trend.

Professional Connections

Decisions in 1939 probably disguised, although reinforcing and symbolizing, another long-term trend in Methodist connectionalism, namely, its reliance upon professions, professionalism, and professional association. What 1939 disguised with the new jurisdictional structures and its ratification of full laity representation was the way in which conference structures, particularly annual conferences, had evolved into professional organizations.[32] Conferences increasingly functioned for clergy the way the state bar did for lawyers. They set standards, reviewed credentials, admitted to practice, guarded prerogative, pressed for compensation, contracted for health care, maintained pensions, and oversaw professional ethics. Coincidentally, conference professionalism continued and grew even as conferences became representative and laypeople were included. Professional interests and concerns, once cared for in annual or General Conference sessions, now lodged in boards or committees (particularly ordained ministry), executive sessions, and various clergy-only affairs. Noting the function of annual conferences as professional organizations for clergy perhaps helps explain why persons who labored under the title of "diaconal ministers" found that lay status insufficient professional recognition and pressed for the status of deacon. Religious educators, church musicians, and other highly trained and well-credentialed professionals now have in the office of permanent deacon and the Order of Deacons the church's affirmation of their professional status (ordination, conference membership, full connection).

Professionalism was by no means limited to conference. Indeed, many sectors of Methodist leadership gradually developed professional patterns, including particularly the extension ministries. For instance, urban missions, settlement houses, urban volunteers, and deaconesses were affected by professionalism; and these prophetic initiatives yielded deaconesses and eventually the new profession of social work.[33] Robert Monk has noted that campus chaplaincy gradually took on a professional aspect.[34] The same might even more readily be demonstrated for other forms of chaplaincy, especially military and hospital chaplaincy. Each role or vocational niche in the church seemed to acquire a professional aspect. Persons in that calling gathered together in regional and national meetings; and, once organized, they sought denominational recognition and/or relation to some board or agency. New and old offices created new professional or quasi-professional associations, new networks that connected the church to offer or receive the special expertise and counsel. So, various church professionals—Christian educators, lay workers, evangelists, missionaries, information officers, large-church pastors, musicians, fiscal officers, church and society persons, and (after 1968) council directors—gathered from across the country in annual, professional, or professional-like meetings. What they sought was comparable to what other professional groupings sought when assembled: how to become more effective in the particular service to which they had been called; how to be better leaders; and how to offer the church the guidance or counsel that they alone could give. The connection was well served by such professionalism. *And* the church was connected through these professional networks, the service they offered for the whole, and by their very existence as the religious counterparts to the webs that held American society together, namely, the professional association.

The servant-character of Methodist professionalism—indeed, of professionalism generally—yields an ambiguous, even self-contradictory relation to conference structures and lay attitudes. Professionals exert influence and lead out of expertise, specialized skills, and privileged knowledge. The church at one moment honors and requires such human elitism and in the next moment reminds itself of the priesthood of all believers, the sinfulness of all, and the gifted nature of truly gracious leadership. Charisma and dependence upon God, not professional skills, it knows, characterize the true servants of God. Ambiguity, distance, even conflict over professional expertise, underlie some of the strains in connectional affairs and, in particular, the marginalization of those professionals whose professional identity, membership, authority, and credentialing lie somewhere else other than in the annual conference.

Some of the conflict draws on ideological or structural concerns as well as professional distance, as, for instance, in the church's concern with Methodist higher and theological education.[35] Charges of liberalism or moral laxity expressively conveyed the sentiment that the professional but Methodist leadership of these institutions had not kept the faith. The 1960s and 1970s brought campus ministry and its politicized connections—indeed, Methodist connectionalism as a whole—into crisis. An increasingly professionally minded campus ministry kept pace with the ideological shifts, moral passion, eager advocacy, and political interventionism of student leadership and higher education generally on matters of race and war, to the consternation of much of the church at large.[36] Similar strains emerged between local Methodism and the "liberal" leaders and program orientation of some of the national boards. "Professionalism" as such did not cause the concern or conflict, but it did effectively "house" Methodist leaders in different networks and thus made communication and problem solving more difficult. Campus ministers at home in meetings with other chaplains and free to express their political views in those settings would not feel as free or be as welcome in an annual conference debating a resolution condemning the moral laxity and political orientation of their school.

The fact that annual conferences themselves function as both representative bodies (lay delegates and ministers coming together from their local churches) *and* the professional association for clergy has perhaps made it difficult for Methodism to recognize the way professionalism both unites and divides. Ministers under regular appointment know in some instinctive, unarticulated way that their membership in annual conference differs from membership in extension relation in more than the manner of appointment. Extension ministers "belong" elsewhere even though by *Discipline* they are still full members of conference and obliged to various kinds of reporting. So a professionalism that brings together educators, chaplains, and other extension ministers into distinct associations both webs the church with new connective fiber and creates divisions between extension ministers and ministers in regular appointment. Indeed, it fosters this dynamic among extension ministries themselves. As I noted in the introduction, I am reminded of that reality every year at our annual extension ministries breakfast. As each member present rises and states his or her position—military chaplain, campus minister, teacher, administrator of our institutions, hospital chaplain, connectional officer—I know I will see none of them again until the next year. For we share virtually nothing except our appointments beyond the local church. Or, more properly, our various identities constitute professional groupings with their own entry procedures, professional meetings, duties and responsibilities, practices and skill sets, connectional networks, publications, and ethical expectations. The church chooses to group us into one category by negative reference.

Post-Corporate Connectionalism

The three dominant styles of twentieth-century connectionalism—corporate, federal, and professional—are under siege. Attacks on agencies, centralized governance of any sort, and elitism are not Methodist-specific but are paralleled in other denominations, large-scale business enterprises, and government at all levels. Apparently, Americans have tired of working in, under, and through corporate, bureaucratic structures. They have tired of having the shots called at national or even conference headquarters. They are done kowtowing to experts. They protest in various ways—taxpayer revolts, rebellions against headquarters, "voting the rascals out," and dropping out.

Organizations respond by downsizing, outsourcing, adopting new schemes of management, and resorting to new measures of influence—regulation, grant making, franchising, consulting, and credentialing. These tactics work, at least in the short run. Virtually every one of these approaches has found its way into denominational repertoire. So United Methodists find themselves offered various franchise opportunities by boards and agencies, Disciple Bible Study being the most successful enterprise. Many individual fans and congregational adoptees of Disciple or Walk to Emmaus would be surprised to discover that it comes from one of United Methodism's corporate entities. The few such successful ventures in franchising, grant making, and consulting do not "redeem" the boards and agencies but instead seem to dissociate themselves from agency programs and so do little to bolster goodwill toward the connectional structures.[37]

Other tactics in organizational vogue—particularly those more controlling, intrusive, accountability prepossessed, and regulatory—do not meet with such favor. Indeed, they both foster and function with an enervating suspicion. Their efforts to make the system work and to command the funds necessary for effective functioning are met with hostility and suspicion. And boards, committees, commissions, and task forces function in an atmosphere where accountability is the first order of business, every slate is immediately assessed for its representativeness, suspicion reigns that money is not being equitably or properly expended, and leadership is experienced only as power. Balkanization reigns in church as in American politics.

The balkanization of United Methodism is displayed in a relatively new form of organization within the church and exacerbated by a growing localism, each of which deserves comment for its important implications for extension ministry. The first is the emergence of caucuses. The second is the redefinition of the purpose and mission of The United Methodist Church (UMC) in relation to the local church. Both of these strong impulses at best ignore and at worst marginalize ministries that extend beyond their circumscribed sense of what matters.

Caucuses

Particularity in Methodism has a long history. In the early twentieth century, Methodism divided its ministries and church order into ethnic-language conferences. The greatest number, of course, were white and English speaking. But still in the 1920s, the MEC had ten German conferences, six Swedish, two Norwegian-Danish, two Hispanic, a Japanese, a Chinese, and twenty African American conferences (plus missions and mission conferences abroad). The MECS lacked the African American conferences but did feature Native American, Hispanic, and German mission conferences. The MPC had African American, German, and Native American conferences. Of course, the EUB and its conferences represented two German-speaking traditions, and at places the language remained very much alive.

However, the twentieth-century project, at least until the 1970s, seemed to be to devalue ethnicity, terminate ministries confined by language and racial lines, and eliminate conference structured for such particular purposes. In some respects this process proceeded gradually as ethnicities declined and congregations, members, and ministers found a home under English-speaking auspices. The anti-German hysteria during and after World War I and Methodist agonies over the segregated and racist Central Jurisdiction accelerated the church's aversion to conferences defined by race and ethnicity. By the 1970s, the Rio Grande Conference, the Puerto Rico Conference,[38] and the Oklahoma Indian Missionary Conference remained as testimony to the importance the churches once accorded conference particularity.

Interestingly, inclusion and unity bred new alternative quasi-conferences. African Americans, faced with abandoning the Central Jurisdiction's structures and prerogatives and merging into white or predominantly white conferences, were among the first to reestablish another members-only form of conference—the caucus. And they were to be among the intended beneficiaries of a new modality of connectionalism, what in American society generally would be known as the monitoring or regulatory agency. Black Methodists for Church Renewal (BMCR) dates from a national organizing conference in February 1968, which in the mood of Black Power, called for self-definition, self-determination, and black solidarity.[39] In that same year, General Conference established the Commission on Religion and Race as a general agency for the new church.

Black Methodists for Church Renewal and, to a lesser extent, the Commission on Religion and Race (which had a multiethnic mandate), continued and gave fresh expression to the conference and connectional life that African Americans had experienced in the Central Jurisdiction. And they signaled what would be a common pattern for the remainder of the century, namely, the emergence of affinity groups, organized locally, on a conference level, regionally, and nationally.

Other groups and commissions, with similarly particularized agendas and membership, emerged at about the same time. Some, like the Good News Movement (1966), remained an association, while others, like the Commission on the Status and Role of Women (COSROW) (1970), gained agency status. The Native American International Caucus saw the light in the same year COSROW was established.[40] Methodists Associated Representing the Cause of Hispanic Americans[41] (MARCHA) was formed in 1971, and in 1974 the National Federation of Asian American United Methodists[42] came into being. Affirmation, a gay and lesbian caucus, emerged in 1975.

The new bodies—whether organized from the affinity group as a caucus or accorded commission status by the denomination—often orient themselves in a prophetic relation to conferences and the rest of the church. They behave like monitoring, watchdog, advocacy, special interest agencies—the religious counterpart to the political action group. Such struggle[43] groups operate with a hermeneutic of suspicion, powers or presumptions of investigation and report, a mandate to correct church policy, and eventually the warrant of official or quasi-official acceptance.

The caucuses have functioned like political action groups. They have also functioned like conference or mission agencies in identifying and developing leadership, urging its recognition by the church as a whole, representing the interests of their membership, demanding the resources requisite for effective ministry and mission, and serving as spokespersons for their membership.

The caucuses function connectionally, becoming alternative Methodist conferences—with conference's revivalistic, "fraternal," and organizational roles. National and regional gatherings feature fervent, celebrative worship, and especially singing. Some groups, like Good News, BMCR, and the Korean caucus, offer explicit and traditional revivalistic fare more in touch with conference's revivalistic heritage than annual conferences themselves. Others experiment liturgically but with comparable intensity, joy, involvement, and expressiveness. The Korean caucus's spirituality functions to continue the transformation of revival into word. The intense spirituality affects the quality of the relationships within and among the group. Gatherings evidence the joyful hugs of meeting and the painful physical parting of early conferences. Individuals network with brothers or sisters sharing the cause, culture, heritage, or language. Publications, phone calls, and computer connections sustain those networks between meetings. Such communalism, ecclesial and eucharistic, furthers Methodism's search for connective tissue—for new styles, modes, and structures of reclaiming the strong affective dimension once characteristic of preacher-only conference meetings. Sometimes such search for a new order seems to be the preoccupation of the affinity groups. At times, they seem consumed with a passion for order, for polity. They envision a new church. Toward that end, collectively the members dream, plan, and labor in building effective and faithful institutions. The caucus may itself be structured to model the new order; or it may devote its energies to structuring United Methodism as a whole. They typically garner resources to institutionalize and to staff for such programming. Caucuses have become expressions of Methodist connectionalism (though, of course and obviously, they divide as well as unite).

The Local Church

In 1996 the *Discipline* began a section on "Organization and Administration" with a treatment of "The Local Church" and started that with a mission statement that reads like and was taken to be the mission of UMC as a whole: "The mission of the Church is to make disciples of Jesus Christ. Local churches provide the most significant arena through which disciple-making occurs."[44]

The *Discipline* has now removed any confusion and relocated that local church-aggrandizing statement to head and begin its treatment of "The Ministry of All Christians," the first section of which is "The Mission and Ministry of the Church."[45] The collapse of the 1784 mission from reforming the continent and spreading scriptural holiness over these lands to local disciple making deserves a chapter, indeed, a book in its own right. Suffice it to say that the focus upon the local church came gradually. In 1928 the MEC bishops recognized the local church as a new norm for Methodism by organizing their address to General Conference around it. They titled the first, long section "The Local Church and What It May Ask of General Methodism." They affirmed:

> The local church is taken as the unit in our study of denominational progress, for it is there that we are to test the value of our organization and polity. It is the point of Methodism's contact with humanity. It is our recruiting office for the King's service. It is for us the institute of religious technology, our workshop, our training camp, our spiritual hospital, our home.[46]

The bishops sustained the military metaphor to describe local Methodism's institutionalization ("training camp," "recruiting office," "point of contact," "service") and nuanced other terms ("hospital," "workshop," "technology") with military force. They devoted major subsections to the church building, members (of all ages), finances, the office, the pastor and pastoral office, laity, and educational institutions (within which they discussed the whole range of Methodist schools and colleges, not just local or intra-church education). In the next major section, the episcopal leaders explored "What the Local Church Owes to General Methodism," only then turning to "What World-Wide Methodism Asks of the World" and "What World-Wide

Methodism Owes to the World." In the first two sections, the bishops had embraced Methodism within the local church; in the latter two, they revisited major issues in relation to national bureaucracy.

Such episcopal statements played a vital role in the long process of obliterating the connectional principle that had once knit Methodism into a series of gatherings, such as band, class, quarterly conference, annual conference, and General Conference. This connectional principle was replaced with a series of corporate structures—local church, district office, conference staff and agencies (jurisdictional staff?), and national boards and agencies. The *Discipline* gradually recognized the linguistic changes and institutional realities. For instance, in 1920, the church quietly interred the quarterly conference with a constitutional amendment that changed "Quarterly" to "Local."[47]

In 1940, as one of the first acts of the newly jurisdictioned and united Methodism, the General Conference authorized the incorporation into one section of the *Discipline* all the various references to local Methodism that had been described under the many rubrics and aspects of Methodism's work:

> Motion of Alfred F. Hughes (West Wisconsin), duly seconded, prevailed that the Editors of the *Discipline* be instructed to bring together in one Section of the *Discipline* legislation referring specifically to the Organization and Administration of the local Church.

A subsequent motion (referred to the Committee on Publishing Interests) asked the Editors to "[c]onsider publishing an inexpensive edition of said *Discipline* containing only those assembled Sections referring to the Local Church."[48]

The church achieved such salience for that part of the *Discipline* without dropping out everything else. With the 1944 *Discipline*, "The Local Church" became Part II of the *Discipline*, immediately following "The Constitution" and preceding Part III, "The Ministry" and Part IV, "The Conferences." In the 1968 *Discipline*, "The Local Church" stood first, embracing even calendar, thus incorporating Methodist time into a congregational orbit. And in 1976 that section expanded to include the discussion of ministry, a symbolical reframing of Wesleyan horizons. Strangely, when it established the new office of permanent deacon, the church tethered its responsibilities for service and witness in the world, defining them negatively as "beyond the local church," effectively construing the norms for even this ministry in congregational terms.[49] Wesley had spoken of the world as his parish; now Methodism indeed has made parish its world.[50] Was this the end to which Wesley intended itinerancy or just the end of itinerancy?

At the very least, the intense focus upon the local church and the powerful dynamic of the ethnic, ideological, and cause caucuses beyond the local church combine to reinforce the marginalization of extension ministries. The latter ministries have removed themselves, or seem removed, from where the action is—in the local church and in caucus politics. Of course, the extension minister can play in both scenes. However, he or she does so not in his or her professional capacity as chaplain or faculty member or administrator but insofar as he or she participates like any layperson in local church or caucus. A mission tied to the local church and organizational life geared to caucuses effectively leaves out extension ministry.

AFTERWORD

Methodism behaves in certain ways like other connectional churches, sharing with them, for instance, the crises, uncertainties, and inner turmoil outlined above as "post-corporate connectionalism." However, Methodism, at least in its better historical moments, has understood its connectionalism as something other than just a polity classification or a strong corporate, centralized, or hierarchical authority system; it has treated connectionalism as something complex and variegated.

Indeed, Methodism has had a changing connectional covenant—differing forms or styles of connectionalism that have emerged over the history of American Methodism. The seven forms of connectionalism that have emerged, each with its distinctive organizational style and all but the last arguably an expression of extension ministry, have been judged for their day and for the Methodism of their day as appropriate measures in enunciating and achieving corporate purposes:

Wesleyan (episcopal)	oral/aural
popular	event
voluntary	printed page
corporate	program
professional	guidance
federal	governance
post-corporate	accountability

In its own way, each style sought to define corporate praxis (a piety and an ecclesiology), to provide mechanisms for collective hearing (our doctrine), to delineate an organizational language (an ecclesial vision), to orient Methodists toward goals (a mission), and to call forth effort (covenant and ethic). Some of these served better and more faithfully as theology in practice—as "practical divinity"—than others. And, at this point, none seems quite adequate, including particularly the style we have awkwardly labeled "post-corporate."

As we think and act toward a new connectional vision, to recognize that connection has changed and that extension ministries (at least in the past) have contributed materially to those changes, just might help us get our bearings.

Perhaps even more transformative and reorienting would be to lessen our preoccupation with denominational structure and fixing it to favor our political stance, and rather to allow ourselves to be refocused by the hymns sung by Mary and versed afresh for us by Charles Wesley. The glory of God! Now there's a mission statement. Mary sings of God's glory, recounting the great things done for the people of God and for her, his servant. Charles bids us sing of God's glory, recalling God's dwelling with Mary and the sending of the "Lord from above." For both, the human prospect lies in the promise of the Spirit.

> O wouldst thou again be made known!
> Again in thy Spirit descend,
> And set up in each of thine own
> A kingdom that never shall end.

These terse little gospels reorient us by calling first for giving God the glory. (Our Presbyterian and Reformed brothers and sisters began their Christian formation by learning the Westminster Catechism, which queries at the very first "What is the chief end of man?" and prompts the answer "Man's chief end is to glorify God, and to enjoy him for ever."[51]) Acknowledging the great things God has done and magnifying the Lord for favoring us with the Spirit permits us to believe that heaven may again be opened on earth. To that end we might recall the full version of American Methodism's first mission statement. It too frames high purpose doxologically:

> *Quest.* 3. What may we reasonably believe to be God's Design, in raising up the Preachers called Methodists?
> *Answ.* To reform the Continent, and spread scripture Holiness over these Lands. As a Proof hereof, we have seen in the Course of fifteen Years a great and glorious Work of God, from New-York through the Jersies, Pennsylvania, Maryland, Virginia, North and South Carolina, even to Georgia.[52]

The first part of the answer we cite often. The second we forget or don't know. It lacks the poignancy of the Magnificat and the elegance of Wesley's verse. But in its own way it focuses attention away from what *we* might do in reforming and spreading and onto what makes our effort possible—*God's* design and *God's* glorious work. As good Arminians we Methodists knew then and should know now that our agency matters. If human effort rests on God's grace, then the first word might be about God's glory.

5

Thinking About Thinking About Extension Ministry

Ephesians 2:1-22

[1]You were dead through the trespasses and sins [2]in which you once lived, following the course of this world, following the ruler of the power of the air, the spirit that is now at work among those who are disobedient. [3]All of us once lived among them in the passions of our flesh, following the desires of flesh and senses, and we were by nature children of wrath, like everyone else. [4]But God, who is rich in mercy, out of the great love with which he loved us [5]even when we were dead through our trespasses, made us alive together with Christ—by grace you have been saved—[6]and raised us up with him and seated us with him in the heavenly places in Christ Jesus, [7]so that in the ages to come he might show the immeasurable riches of his grace in kindness toward us in Christ Jesus. [8]For by grace you have been saved through faith, and this is not your own doing; it is the gift of God—[9]not the result of works, so that no one may boast. [10]For we are what he has made us, created in Christ Jesus for good works, which God prepared beforehand to be our way of life.

[11]So then, remember that at one time you Gentiles by birth, called "the uncircumcision" by those who are called "the circumcision"—a physical circumcision made in the flesh by human hands—[12]remember that you were at that time without Christ, being aliens from the commonwealth of Israel, and strangers to the covenants of promise, having no hope and without God in the world. [13]But now in Christ Jesus you who once were far off have been brought near by the blood of Christ. [14]For he is our peace; in his flesh he has made both groups into one and has broken down the dividing wall, that is, the hostility

between us. [15]He has abolished the law with its commandments and ordinances, that he might create in himself one new humanity in place of the two, thus making peace, [16]and might reconcile both groups to God in one body through the cross, thus putting to death that hostility through it. [17]So he came and proclaimed peace to you who were far off and peace to those who were near; [18]for through him both of us have access in one Spirit to the Father. [19]So then you are no longer strangers and aliens, but you are citizens with the saints and also members of the household of God, [20]built upon the foundation of the apostles and prophets, with Christ Jesus himself as the cornerstone. [21]In him the whole structure is joined together and grows into a holy temple in the Lord; [22]in whom you also are built together spiritually into a dwelling place for God.

—⚮—

1 Captain of Israel's host, and guide[1]
      Of all who seek the land above,
   Beneath thy shadow we abide,
      The cloud of thy protecting love:
   Our strength, thy grace; our rule, thy Word;
   Our end, the glory of the Lord.

2 By thy unerring Spirit led,
      We shall not in the desert stray;
   We shall not full direction need,
      Or miss our providential way;
   As far from danger as from fear,
   While love, almighty love, is near.

This chapter offers several resources for reflecting with integrity about extension ministry and about its relation to United Methodist ministry as a whole. I begin with a set of assumptions that help us think about ministry, focused particularly for consideration of extension ministry. I then present in schematic outline an interpretive model for thinking theologically and missionally about extension ministry within the larger understanding of Christian ministry generally and United Methodist ministry particularly. I have outlined the schema using the Wesleyan quadrilateral.[2] The chapter concludes with questions for further reflection.

As the reader will discover, the suggestions, hypotheses, queries, and convictions offered here have governed earlier chapters. I suppose I might have positioned this chapter earlier. However, given the somewhat abstract and probing character of the reflections below, it seems to make sense to hold them until after the reader has been engaged in such thinking, at least implicitly, in the foregoing chapters. So, first some assumptions, then an extended theological schema—the heart of the chapter—and, finally, some questions.

ASSUMPTIONS

As United Methodists, we instinctively move to address ecclesial and ministry problems structurally and organizationally, that is, as a polity or Disciplinary matter. This is an appropriate and faithful action when such ordering or reordering is undertaken with a sense of our theological and biblical bearings—in short, when we "practice" our theology. Sometimes, however, political or economic interests overwhelm and distort decision making, effectively eroding or eclipsing its theologically reflective dimension. To orient reconsideration of the place of extension ministries within the overall United Methodist framework and to do so with a sense of our theological bearings, I propose the following assumptions:

1. No matter how much we might wish to enhance extension ministry or how monumental the changes proposed, we do not start afresh to conceive and define the several offices. Instead we work out from ministry as lived in our heritage, from Scripture's witness about leadership, from the wisdom about office and order derived from tradition and mirrored for us in other communions, and from best practices and our best thinking in relation to these givens.

2. Extension ministries are absolutely vital to the American United Methodist connectional pattern and the well-being of our connectional system, the conference system, and the horizons and work of our

congregations. Our ministry as a whole depends upon vital relation with, effective deployment of, and effectiveness of chaplains and other extension ministers.

3. Therefore, a general purpose ought to be to think in terms of and to enhance the whole connection and to strengthen mission and ministry at all levels.

4. In particular, acceptable strengthening of extension ministries ought to strengthen leadership of United Methodism generally.

5. In keeping with traditions inherited from John Wesley, refined through the centuries, and codified in the various *Disciplines*, Methodists and Wesleyans affirm the distinctive leadership roles in all offices—lay, licensed, consecrated, commissioned, ordained, pastoral, and extension—and especially the distinctive callings by Scripture and tradition allocated between and among bishops, elders, and deacons.

6. In rethinking and renewing extension ministry, fresh attention needs to be given to which roles and vocations warrant deacon's and elder's ordination, respectively, and to how extension ministries might relate more constructively, programmatically, and substantively to the orders.

7. Insofar as possible proposals for change ought to reflect our Wesleyan theology and practice of ministry as well (that is, honor what the tradition has understood ministry to be and what, following Wesley, United Methodists affirm about itinerancy, lay ministries, itinerant general superintendency, and conferencing).

8. Reform efforts should be guided by the mission of the church, the well-being of the people called United Methodist, and the effectiveness of our witness to the world.

9. As we probe the nature and purpose of the various extension ministries, we ought to think of the global nature of the church, most specifically our larger communion as represented in the World Methodist Council and more generally with other denominations or ecclesial connections with which we are engaged bilaterally and multilaterally. Alterations in understandings and practices of ministry ought

to move the church toward the unity of the body of Christ for which Jesus prayed and the mission of Christ for the world, the *missio Dei*.

10. We should build as much as possible on prior and current studies of specialized ministries, ministry generally, sacraments, and church order.

11. We concede that, however coherent a vision of a renewed extension ministry and a renewed connection we might develop in this volume, any agenda or proposal that emerges needs testing with United Methodists generally.

REFLECTING THEOLOGICALLY AND MISSIONALLY

Given such assumptions, I offer below a schema including a number of determinants for United Methodist ministerial offices, with a particular eye to North America. In an earlier day, this focus on the North American ministerial scene would not have required a rationale. Indeed, the imperative of speaking as a *united* Methodism to and within the United States constituted one of the significant motivations for the union of 1939 that produced The Methodist Church. Now in a church whose membership growth increasingly occurs beyond North America, United Methodist leaders—bishops and agency staff particularly—accent the global nature of our church. I appreciate this self-understanding and the reality of our broader connectionalism, as the eighth assumption above affirms.

However, with respect to ministries, and especially extension ministries, we need to recognize the critically important reality of context, time, and circumstance. Ministry does and must configure itself in relation to language, culture, society, and politics. It can—and, sadly, often does—overly conform, "following the course of this world." It becomes servant to fashions, powers, and loyalties of society and culture. It reverts to the deadness from which the apostle Paul declared that we have been liberated.

However, if conformity must be avoided, so also must the other extreme: removal, avoidance, irrelevance, and isolation. At our best, Methodists have been neither cultural conformists nor sectarians. Rather, we have sought to transform: "To reform the Continent, and spread scripture Holiness over these Lands." And, again at our best, we have done so with the understanding that ministry is cruciform, incarnational, pneumatological, and missional. Methodist ministry, including extension ministry, operates and abides beneath God's shadow, led by the Spirit, and conforming to Christ: "Our strength, thy grace; our rule, thy word; / Our end, the glory of the Lord."

The following schema and its individual determinants and norms recognize the time- and context-specific character of ministry. Some of these determinants have a received, principled, and even fixed quality. Others function to generate openness to experimentation and change. A case can be made for these criteria to have continually shaped and reshaped Methodist ministry; for the schema is, in fact, the quadrilateral by which Methodists are supposed to take reflective action. However, it has been only recently that we have become self-conscious about quadrilateral ways of theologizing. And since the "discovery" of the quadrilateral (as well as before), Methodists have sometimes made quite dramatic changes to ministry and connection with at best quite fleeting glances at Scripture and tradition and a few times without good reason (in a very few instances perhaps one could say, "out of their minds"). Greater self-consciousness in decision making would make it possible for us to bring about more faithful and effective forms of ministry and to find ways of putting extension and itinerant ministry back together and determining which extension roles belong appropriately to the diaconate.

Here, then, I offer a framework for thinking about extension ministry with the delivery elements of the quadrilateral distinguished and their freight identified. In decision making and in thinking about church and ministry we would not, I trust, proceed so woodenly through the authorities. Indeed, to do so would not be thinking quadrilaterally. We do not, for instance, get to Scripture or honor its primacy without employing the other elements of the quadrilateral. We employ our minds to read or hear (reason). We understand a biblical passage with categories, doctrines, creedal affirmations, metaphors, mental pictures, and convictions that tradition has given us. And both Scripture and tradition have been mediated through Vacation Bible School story telling, dramatic Christmas pageants, youth retreats, parental admonition, and relations with pastors and teachers—in short, mediated through our own experience and that of others around us.

So the schema, first in outline and then in outline extended:

Scripture: The Bible and extension ministry
Reason: The Wesleyan charism (roles, scripts, structures, and processes)
Experience: Extension ministry as lived (with particular attention to North America and Methodist experience)
  • Functional or pragmatic dictates
  • American democratic protocols
  • Contemporary leadership patterns
  • The Methodist experience
Tradition: The ancient and ecumenical witness

I believe that thinking about thinking about ministry requires the full resources of Wesleyan theologizing. I concede that positing relations or equations between elements of the quadrilateral and specific sets of norms has something of an artificial quality. The normative freight associated with Scripture and experience should not raise eyebrows. However, the connection of the Wesleyan charism with reason and of tradition with the ecumenical witness may seem less obvious. One can certainly make the case that we ought to connect the Wesleyan contribution with either or both tradition and experience, recognizing Wesley's tutelage as shaping our tradition and as experientially conceived and lived into. Earlier chapters accord with such construals, illustrated in my use in this volume of Wesley hymns (along with Scripture) and my probing of our American Wesleyan experience. Here I associate the Wesleyan charism with reason because it provides the categories in terms of which we think about ministry. Similarly, it has been Methodist involvement with the ecumenical movement and the broad liturgical renewal that has made us conscious afresh of the early church and of the Wesleys' own deep indebtedness to early and eastern Christianity. Out of our engagement in and contributions to the ecumenical and liturgical efforts of the twentieth century have come the categories and understandings that now shape our worship, ecclesiology, and ministry. However, I would not object if the reader prefers to ignore the associations I have just explained or to move them around (for instance, putting the Wesley section under tradition or experience and considering reason to be a delivery mechanism).

Nor would I object if the reader counters that quadrilateral reflection ought to govern consideration of all norms and determinants rather than be equated with any specific set. However, I do find the schema below helpful in calling attention to the several norms that are important in our reflection about extension ministry. Viewing them together should keep us from allowing them to function independently, which, unfortunately, too often has been our pattern.

QUADRILATERAL NORMS FOR MINISTRY

Scripture: The Bible and Extension Ministry

- Christ's ministry (Prophet, Priest, and King)—the cruciform nature of ministry and of leadership, the importance of all three of Christ's traditional offices, implications for extension ministry of each
- Focus: proclamation of the Kingdom, the good news, the promise of redemption, the call to discipleship, the mandate to preach the gospel
- Apostolic pattern(s) of healing, reconciliation, teaching
- Biblical injunctions to minister to the poor, the outcast, the persecuted, and ministry as therefore so shaped
- Explicit New Testament teaching on the orders of ministry
- The varieties of gifts, one Spirit

Reason: The Wesleyan Charism
(roles, scripts, structures, and processes)

- The leadership style(s) and norm(s) exemplified by John Wesley and Francis Asbury

- Itinerancy and extension roles
- A distinctive recovery of apostolic leadership—ministry as missional, evangelistic, sent, appointed/appointive

Wesley's extension roles (as already elaborated)

- A pneumatological understanding of ministry, including extension ministries
- Extension ministries as creators/creatures of connection
- Leadership and involvement in conference
- Exercise of appointment and its bearing on extension roles
- Extension ministers as bearers of Methodism's holiness doctrines, witnesses to social holiness, and strategists of mission

Experience: Extension Ministry as Lived (with particular attention to North America and Methodist experience)

Functional or pragmatic dictates (societal determinants)

- Professional expectations, behavioral norms, codes of conduct and vocational patterns peculiar to each form of extension ministry
- Employer codes, expectations, rules, and guidelines
- The (extension) ministerial office as shaped by and shaping training and educational programs peculiar to it
- Best practices—management and good business expectations, accountability and transparency, administrative effectiveness, financial management and fiscal integrity, supervisory and reporting norms
- Societal openness to the generation of new roles, offices, techniques, communication styles, media
- Extension ministry as modeled and shaped by its practitioners, especially by those who extend its work and refashion it

American democratic protocols (political determinants)

- Pressures on extension ministry from civil political practice where election of leadership, participation in decision making, free speech and free press, accountability and openness apply

- Expectations about equality and fairness (on salary, status, authority, perks)
- The invocation of "rights" and "rights" language, especially as pertaining to access to forms of ministry, to promotions and assignments, and to elevation to leadership
- Tensions between democratizing, participatory, and lay expectations of the governance, involvement, authorization, and exercise of extension ministries *and* the expertise, skill, peculiar knowledge, and professionalism of the extension ministry in question

Contemporary leadership patterns (leadership determinants)

- Prevalent and celebrated business patterns (e.g., servant leadership)
- Leadership models adopted within ministry (e.g., executive ministry, mega-church)
- Culture and media patterns (the media-savvy, contemporary culture-sensitive preacher and worship leader
- Implications of the shift toward a local church and diocesan mode for extension ministries—administration, budgetary roles, pastoral oversight, problem solving

The Methodist experience (Methodist-specific determinants)

- Models and evolution of Wesleyan-style leadership (itinerancy, rhythms, work, expectations, residency)
- Contribution to and adaptations from societal leadership styles and consequent evolution of the ministerial and extension ministerial offices
- Extension ministers as strategists—the missionary, evangelistic, envisioning, initiative-taking roles
- Evolving covenantal patterns (from the itinerant covenant to today's Christian conferencing and covenant groups)
- Changing relations to General Conference and particularly to annual conferences
- The office as shaped by the procedures for entering it

- The *Discipline*'s explicit mandates on extension ministry and on the deacon and the elder
- Trajectories out of current (including personal) experience

Tradition: The ancient and ecumenical witness

- The threefold pattern of ministry (bishop, elder, deacon)—in Scripture, in the traditions of the churches, and as ecumenical norm[3]
- Extension ministry as sacramental, pastoral, teaching, but also as witnessing to love and justice
- Fresh understandings of the deacon from bilateral and multilateral dialogues
- Servants of the whole church
- Recovery of the teaching office
- The office configured and exercised so as to further Methodism's ecumenical commitments and hopes

An exhortation from these norms then as we reflect and strategize about United Methodist ministry as a whole and of the role and place of extension ministries within it. WE OUGHT TO BE:

- faithful to Scripture, the Wesleyan norms, and the *Book of Discipline.*
- instructed by our experience—with itinerancy and ministry generally.
- cognizant of best practices of leadership, teaching, and ministry.
- drawn by our vision of the kingdom of God and our hope for the unity of Christ's church.
- committed to and oriented by the church's apostolic witness.

QUESTIONS

I suggest the questions below as helpful in thinking about extension ministry—whether it might be reshaped and how the distance between extension and regular itinerancy might be lessened. My hope is that these questions will generate further queries that groups concerned with reordering our ministries might entertain.

1. How might the norms outlined above and the exposition in earlier chapters change our understanding of extension ministry and our sense of what this ministry might be for United Methodism and its mission?
2. Would an enhanced conception of extension ministry provide further clarity for United Methodism about its mission and its mission statement?
3. What does the church (and the world) need from its leaders?
4. What parts of that mandate ought to lie with those in extension ministries? with deacons? with elders?
5. If the aim is to strengthen extension ministry in its function with and relation to United Methodism as a whole, with respect to what aspects or dimensions of the connection's nature and work?
6. Is there a vision of the office of extension ministry that ought to guide strategizing and thinking?
7. What aspects of these ministries ought to be accented?
    * the teaching office?
    * missional/strategic responsibilities?
    * relation to administrative, appointive authority?
    * connectional roles?
    * leadership through institutional structures?
    * sacramental and pastoral dimensions?
    * responsibility for the unity of and apostolic witness of the church?
8. How well developed is a United Methodist theology of extension ministry?
    * If fully articulated, does it embrace extension roles generally or does it focus primarily on one style of extension ministry?
    * If crafted dogmatically, how adequate is this theology?
    * If enacted and lived, where is this theology best exemplified and how might the church and extension ministers tease out the theological presumptions and implications?
    * How fully and well do the United Methodist practice and theology of ministry come to focus in extension roles?

- Where is United Methodist understanding of ministry best institutionalized and/or theologized?
9. How should we conceive of extension ministries in relation to the church's ministry as a whole?
   - What aspects must be represented in the elder's office?
   - What aspects charged especially to deacons?
   - What aspects shared with the whole people of God?
   - What aspects distributed among the various ministerial offices?
10. With respect to leadership roles:
    - Which roles need to be focused in and exercised by pastoral or local ministries?
    - Which roles can be readily shared with those in extension roles?
11. What aspects of extension ministries most need attention?
    - The specific exercise of their offices?
    - Their relation to annual conferences?
    - Their relation to local churches?
    - Their connection to "the connection," including boards and agencies?
    - Their roles as teachers and witnesses to the world?
12. What changes in the role or office would be most conducive to the leadership that the church needs?

For persons already exercising extension ministry

1. What inquiries, consultations, working groups, and conversations do you need to generate new or reclaimed agendas?
2. In approaching your work, do you start with theological and missional convictions or are financial, structural, or workload issues too pressing to be put off?
   - If the latter, can you understand and permit attention to practicalities and practice as itself a theological endeavor?
   - Or will you begin by probing for and discerning the theological implications of your present practice of ministry?

3. What might be the theological freight of ministry as you attempt to reorder it?

—⚊—

The upshot of these questions is, what is to be done? To that concern we return in the next and concluding chapter.

AFTERWORD

The biblical text and the hymn at the outset of this chapter should remind us that in the exercise of ministry we do so faithfully only through God's grace, through heeding God's Word, by keeping ourselves servant to Christ, and by remaining always alert to the guidance of the Spirit. Charles Wesley puts it well: "Our strength, thy grace; our rule, thy word; / Our end, the glory of the Lord." Paul agrees: "For by grace you have been saved through faith, and this is not your own doing; it is the gift of God—not the result of works, so that no one may boast. For we are what he has made us, created in Christ Jesus for good works, which God prepared beforehand to be our way of life."

Should not the same convictions guide our thinking and strategizing about ministry? Should not our rethinking of extension ministry proceed with full attention to Scripture and with conscious efforts to interpret it alive to the guidance of the Spirit in our own lives (experience) and to the wisdom the Spirit has conveyed through the ages (tradition)? If this is our approach, then we might hear afresh this counsel from the apostle Paul (Eph. 2:19-22):

> So then you are no longer strangers and aliens, but you are citizens with the saints and also members of the household of God, built upon the foundation of the apostles and prophets, with Christ Jesus himself as the cornerstone. In him the whole structure is joined together and grows into a holy temple in the Lord; in whom you also are built together spiritually into a dwelling place for God.

And from Charles Wesley: "Beneath thy shadow we abide, / The cloud of thy protecting love; / By thine unerring Spirit led, / We shall not in the desert stray."

Thinking about thinking about extension ministry should proceed with as much guidance from the Spirit, knowledge of God and of God's Word, and conformity with Christ as we expect and pray for in the exercise of ministry. Thinking about thinking about ministry should take quadrilateral form.

Epilogue

A Word to Extension Ministers

John 17:1-26

[1]After Jesus had spoken these words, he looked up to heaven and said, "Father, the hour has come; glorify your Son so that the Son may glorify you, [2]since you have given him authority over all people, to give eternal life to all whom you have given him. [3]And this is eternal life, that they may know you, the only true God, and Jesus Christ whom you have sent. [4]I glorified you on earth by finishing the work that you gave me to do. [5]So now, Father, glorify me in your own presence with the glory that I had in your presence before the world existed.

[6]"I have made your name known to those whom you gave me from the world. They were yours, and you gave them to me, and they have kept your word. [7]Now they know that everything you have given me is from you; [8]for the words that you gave to me I have given to them, and they have received them and know in truth that I came from you; and they have believed that you sent me. [9]I am asking on their behalf; I am not asking on behalf of the world, but on behalf of those whom you gave me, because they are yours. [10]All mine are yours, and yours are mine; and I have been glorified in them. [11]And now I am no longer in the world, but they are in the world, and I am coming to you. Holy Father, protect them in your name that you have given me, so that they may be one, as we are one. [12]While I was with them, I protected them in your name that you have given me. I guarded them, and not one of them was lost except the one destined to be lost, so that the scripture might be fulfilled. [13]But now I am coming to you, and I speak these things in the world so that they may have my joy made complete in themselves. [14]I have given them your word, and the world has hated

them because they do not belong to the world, just as I do not belong to the world. [15]I am not asking you to take them out of the world, but I ask you to protect them from the evil one. [16]They do not belong to the world, just as I do not belong to the world. [17]Sanctify them in the truth; your word is truth. [18]As you have sent me into the world, so I have sent them into the world. [19]And for their sakes I sanctify myself, so that they also may be sanctified in truth.

[20]"I ask not only on behalf of these, but also on behalf of those who will believe in me through their word, [21]that they may all be one. As you, Father, are in me and I am in you, may they also be in us, so that the world may believe that you have sent me. [22]The glory that you have given me I have given them, so that they may be one, as we are one, [23]I in them and you in me, that they may become completely one, so that the world may know that you have sent me and have loved them even as you have loved me. [24]Father, I desire that those also, whom you have given me, may be with me where I am, to see my glory, which you have given me because you loved me before the foundation of the world.

[25]"Righteous Father, the world does not know you, but I know you; and these know that you have sent me. [26]I made your name known to them, and I will make it known, so that the love with which you have loved me may be in them, and I in them."

—⟡—

1   Partners of a glorious hope,[1]
    Lift your hearts and voices up.
    Jointly let us rise and sing
    Christ our Prophet, Priest, and King.
    Monuments of Jesu's grace,
    Speak we by our lives his praise,
    Walk in him we have received,
    Show we not in vain believed.

2   While we walk with God in light
    God our hearts doth still unite;
    Dearest fellowship we prove,
    Fellowship in Jesu's love;

Sweetly each with each combined,
In the bonds of duty joined,
Feels the cleansing blood applied,
Daily feels that Christ hath died.

3 Still, O Lord, our faith increase,
Cleanse from all unrighteousness;
Thee th'unholy cannot see,
Make, O make us meet for thee:
Every vile affection kill,
Root out every seed of ill,
Utterly abolish sin,
Write thy law of love within.

4 Hence may all our actions flow,
Love the proof that Christ we know;
Mutual love the token be,
Lord, that we belong to thee.
Love, thine image love impart!
Stamp it on our face and heart!
Only love to us be given—
Lord, we ask no other heaven.

———

Over the course of the twentieth century, extension ministries (those not a part of cabinets) have distanced themselves from or been distanced from the annual conferences, which, theoretically and officially, remain the membership units for clergy and the basic body of the church. In many instances real distance explains the gulf. Clergy find themselves quite removed from their annual conferences when sent into international mission fields, elected to or employed by a Nashville general agency, deployed as a military chaplain to Iraq or Korea, or appointed to an out-of-conference college, seminary, or hospital. Playing a meaningful part in conference life proves quite difficult—impossible, really—for extension ministers so removed from the bounds of the conference. As one who remained in the North Carolina Conference for more than two decades of seminary, graduate school, and teaching in the New York/New Jersey area, I can attest to this difficulty from personal experience. I faithfully attended annual conference sessions and submitted charge conference and annual conference reports, but, given that I lived 500 miles away, I could not participate in local church, district, or conference events.

DISTANCED MINISTRIES

Extension ministers without the excuse of geographical distance—those appointed and serving within the bounds of annual conferences—also distance themselves or are distanced from conference life (again excepting those on cabinets or extended cabinets). Faculty members, hospital chaplains, and clergy serving in other service institutions on a daily basis function in systems parallel to the annual conference, with their own expectations, rules, budgets, rewards, power structures, and authority. As we have seen, many extension ministries constitute distinct professions. Theoretically and officially they belong as well to the clergy profession, functionally represented in United Methodism in the annual conference. Their paychecks, however, orient extension ministers professionally and practically to their employing institution.

Extension ministries do have, again at least theoretically, a professional connection to the church. We might argue that over the course of the twentieth century the churches now constitutive of United Methodism have moved the professional orientation of special, ABLC, or extension ministries from annual conference to the connectional level (and, save for missionaries, to the national level). Extension ministers increasingly have oriented themselves beyond the annual conference to general boards and agencies as their primary referents, standard-setters, credentialers, and resourcers. Chaplains and campus ministers look to the General Board of Higher Education and Ministry (GBHEM) and missionaries refer to the General Board of Global Ministries (GBGM). These two agencies fulfill a gatekeeping and credentialing function vis-à-vis chaplains and missionaries. Other extension ministries have a much looser relation to the connectional level. For instance, colleges and universities and their faculties and administrators relate to GBHEM, while seminary staff and their faculties relate to GBHEM and AUMTS (the Association of United Methodist Theological Schools). Similarly, one might trace the relation of agency staff to the General Council on Finance and Administration (GCFA) and perhaps to the new Connectional Table. None of these connections, certainly not the last, has anything like the accountability and oversight responsibilities that bishops, annual conferences, and boards of ordained ministry exercise with respect to the ordained generally. Indeed, institutions struggle with the question as to what it means to be United Methodist when their employees and constituencies become highly pluralistic. For example, colleges do well to keep United Methodists at the helm and in charge of religious life. They labor to retain the affection and minimal support the church offers. And their highly diverse faculties would not look on matters professional to either GBHEM or to the annual conference.

The professionalization of extension ministries has much to do, then, with their distance from the annual conference and the life and accountability associated with it. As we have seen, distancing has also occurred because of changes in conference itself. The extension minister playing a leadership role in annual conferences is the exception rather than the rule, as was the case in the nineteenth century. It is telling that conferences elect fewer and fewer extension ministers to delegations for General Conference and jurisdictions. Extension ministers relate to conferences now in mediated fashion—through the annual conference structures of accountability, which have been delegated to boards of ordained ministry or committees or special offices.

The forces making for distance between extension minister and conference, then, are many and diverse. They include a number of trends (some of which we have explored):

- sheer growth of conferences, in some cases necessitating the move of the annual session out of churches into impersonal convention centers
- admission (for other than Methodist Protestants) into conferences of laity in equal numbers to clergy and the consequent transformation of conferences into representative assemblies

- professionalization of the ministry and particularly of special ministries
- routinization of review of character ("nothing against the clergy on the XX district")
- further centralization of the program and initiative-taking activities of the denomination into boards and agencies
- jurisdictioning of the U.S. connection and increased emphasis on The United Methodist Church as a global church
- drift of special appointments into accountability to other institutions
- explosion of numbers of those in such special situations
- the *apotheosis* (elevation to prominence) of the local church
- the consequent gravitation toward understanding "real" ministry as within a local church and everything else as "beyond the local church."

So extension ministries have recently gravitated out of conference life. By making changes in nomenclature and explication recent General Conferences have improved our understanding of such ministries as extending the overall ministry of the church. And annual conferences, under new Disciplinary protocols, have clearly worked at rebuilding the relation of those in extension ministries to the conference. However, we still have not recovered structures and processes that once claimed special ministries—those once exercised by Wesley—as belonging to conference and as intimately connected with all ministry.

Indeed, mechanisms intended to reconnect carry ironic disconnective overtones. Annual reports pose questions about and ask for detail on activities that define and characterize pastoral ministry, not the particular profession of the extension minister. Annual meetings with the bishop or district superintendent contrive for purpose. Special breakfasts at annual conference embrace the extension ministries in a sense, but symbolize more effectively the irrelevance of these ministries to the meeting as a whole. Attendance at annual conference seems less a desired and significant involvement than an act of compliance. Interaction with the annual conference and with the bishops, though intended to connect and achieve accountability, actually signal the marginality of extension ministries and their distance from conference.

OUR RESPONSIBILITY AS EXTENSION MINISTERS

To this point in the book, I have accented the ways in which long-term developments and trends have changed the place of extension ministries within the connection. I would suggest further that up to now those of us in extension or ABLC or special appointment have waited for General Conference or for a general agency (or for divine intervention!) to discern and remedy the situation. Someone else, we seemed to believe, ought to address the problems we present to the appointive process and to reassert our proper place within the connection. Or else we like the "distance" and prefer to keep ours.

What if we extension ministers were to exercise some responsibility in raising the issues and proposing solutions? What if we refused to leave it to someone else to deal with our disconnect and marginality? What if we thought distance a problem and decided to deal with it ourselves?

I offer the queries and proposals below as a way of prompting extension ministers to involve themselves in reform. Although each is intended to work at connection and connectivity, these trial initiatives move in various and occasionally alternative or contradictory directions. (Of course, those not in extension ministry who have labored this far into the book or chapter are certainly invited to think through the issues with us.)

1. Given how structures of connection and accountability and structures for mission have evolved, and given the role previously played by extension ministers themselves in rethinking and reshaping connection:
   - What ought such ministries to look like from now on to make most effective our part in the *missio Dei?*
   - What distinctive roles might those in extension ministries play within United Methodism nationally and globally?
   - How ought such ministries be labeled, defined, and understood within the ordained ministry as a whole?
2. What are extension ministers' responsibility in the church's overall change and transformation and its theological reflection?

- Do extension ministers have a distinctive apprehension of the Wesleyan charism that ought to be shared?
- Do they have helpful perspectives to offer on itinerancy, connection, deacons' and elders' orders, the local ministry?

3. Is the present nomenclature of "extension" satisfactory? If so, would the *Discipline* be more faithful to our Wesleyan heritage if it more consistently employed the new rubrics "appointments extending the ministry of The United Methodist Church" or "appointments within or appointments beyond the connectional structures" and removed entirely the remaining, repeatedly used, and clearly congregationalist or parish notion of "appointments beyond the local church"? Should we attempt to rewrite the sentences and paragraphs?

4. Should offices wholly within present conference structures and determined by episcopal appointment (as, for instance, the posts of district superintendents or conference staff) be removed from the extension category and recognized as genuinely itinerant appointments?

5. Should persons appointed, effectively beyond the connectional structure (not to cabinets or within annual conferences), and whose careers or engagements promise continued employment, surrender or waive guaranteed appointment?
   - Might they be expected to continue to affiliate with their conference or with a conference contiguous to their appointment but with voice and not vote?
   - Might their membership lie in their order (elder or deacon) rather than in the annual conference?
   - What procedures ought then to be established for such persons to request or to reapply for reinstatement for purposes of appointment and itinerancy?

6. Might the notion of "location" be reclaimed and its negative implications removed so as to serve, as it once did, for persons who would remain "deacon" or "elder" but who elect not to function under the expectations and responsibilities of appointment, full connection,

conference, and order membership? For instance, individuals might locate as elders when their setting involves them in a ministry of Word, Sacrament, and Order or when exercise of such roles will be through their membership in Methodist institutions, though ancillary to their job (as, for instance, with a faculty member or administrator at a United Methodist college).

7. Might the church provide for easy transfer of elders into the new permanent diaconate or for such located elders into the local diaconate (or vice versa) if and when their roles come more to approximate that order than the one to which they have been ordained?

8. Should new conference structures be elaborated into which those within the connectional structure and those beyond the connectional structure would be appointed?

   - Might the structure of "central" connectional units again be utilized or some similar rubric generated to provide meaningful conference structures for extension ministries?

   - Might some appointments be made not within annual conferences, but in central districts, when the ministry in question has a trans-local but not trans-conference range and has a strong nexus with district superintendents?

   - Might other appointments be made within new "central" conferences when the ministry has a trans-conference range and has a strong nexus with one or more bishops?

   - Might truly national or transdenominational appointments be made within a "national" or "connectional" jurisdiction?

   - Might such central bodies have rights of representation in the higher regular conference structure (district within the annual conference; annual within a jurisdiction; jurisdiction within the General Conference)?

   - Should the point of such central bodies be not the segregation of those in such special appointments but rather of creating structures of mission and accountability appropriate to the range and character of their ministerial service? (Indeed, the primary utility of such conferences for persons in special appointments would be to recreate something like the review of character—something that would give those conferences a covenant discipleship dimension. So, for instance, a conference of United Methodist hospital chaplains or seminary faculty would serve as both a resourcing and accountability structure.)

9. Should those of us currently included in the extension, ABLC, or special category be zealous in making the Disciplinary accountabilities and affiliations work?

10. Absent significant change, should we work more zealously at our relations with one another and organize with the aim of having some representation in the decision making that affects us?

11. How else might we work to effect meaningful and substantive change in the United Methodist connectional order—change that enhances the whole and our part in it?

AFTERWORD

Throughout the Gospel of John, as evident in the passage opening this chapter, Jesus grounds his ministry in the fact that he is sent by the Father. From his sending by the Father derives the sending of the disciples. Jesus prays for, invokes the Spirit on, commissions, and sends his disciples. John Wesley grasped, exercised himself, and bequeathed to us such an understanding of ministry as being "sent." His brother penned a hymn that prayed to Jesus and echoed his prayer for such commissions (albeit based on Matt. 9:38).

1 LORD of the harvest, hear[2]
   Thy needy servants cry;
 Answer our faith's effectual prayer,
   And all our wants supply.

 2 On Thee we humbly wait;
   Our wants are in Thy view:

The harvest truly, Lord, is great;
    The labourers are few.

  3 Convert, and send forth more
     Into Thy church abroad;
And let them speak Thy word of power,
    As workers with their God.

The hymn reproduced at the beginning of this chapter sounds a related Johannine note, namely, that Christ's followers are to be united in their service. This volume has premised and posited just that hope—that extension ministers and those in the regular itinerancy are "partners of a glorious hope." So I exhort (to use a good Methodist term) that

While we walk with God in light[3]
God our hearts doth still unite;
Dearest fellowship we prove,
Fellowship in Jesu's love;
Sweetly each with each combined,
In the bonds of duty joined,
Feels the cleansing blood applied,
Daily feels that Christ hath died.

I close with two other hymns from Charles Wesley of which I have become quite fond, whose sentiments I would wish on those who have read this far, and whose guidance I believe would helpfully guide those who labor to make our church more faithful. I believe a small part of such a renewal would be aided by a significant recovery of and commissioning of new tunes for the wonderful Wesley verse.

  1 Thy ceaseless, unexhausted love,[4]
     Unmerited and free,
   Delights our evil to remove,
     And help our misery.

  2 Thou waitest to be gracious still;
     Thou dost with sinners bear,

That saved we may thy goodness feel,
 And all thy grace declare.

3 Thy goodness and thy truth to me,
  To every soul, abound,
 A vast, unfathomable sea,
  Where all our thoughts are drowned.

4 Its streams the whole creation reach,
  So plenteous is the store,
 Enough for all, enough for each,
  Enough for evermore!

5 Faithful, O Lord, thy mercies are,
  A rock that cannot move;
 A thousand promises declare
  Thy constancy of love.

6 Throughout the universe it reigns,
  Unalterably sure;
 And while the truth of God remains,
  The goodness must endure.

—⚏—

1 Author of faith, eternal Word,[5]
  Whose Spirit breathes the active flame,
 Faith, like its finisher and Lord,
  Today as yesterday the same;

2 To thee our humble hearts aspire,
  And ask the gift unspeakable;
 Increase in us the kindled fire,
  In us the work of faith fulfil.

3 By faith we know thee strong to save
  (Save us, a present Saviour thou!)

Whate'er we hope, by faith we have,
    Future and past subsisting now.

4 To him that in thy name believes
    Eternal life with thee is given;
Into himself he all receives—
    Pardon, and holiness, and heaven.

5 The things unknown to feeble sense,
    Unseen by reason's glimmering ray,
With strong commanding evidence
    Their heavenly origin display.

6 Faith lends its realizing light,
    The clouds disperse, the shadows fly;
Th'Invisible appears in sight,
    And God is seen by mortal eye.

Notes

Introduction: Mr. Wesley's True Heirs: Extension Ministers

1. This Charles Wesley hymn can be found in *The Methodist Hymn-Book* (London: Wesleyan Conference Office, 1925), 624, #753. Some of the hymns that begin the other chapters are taken from *A Collection of Hymns for the Use of the People Called Methodists*, volume 7 of *The Works of John Wesley*, ed. Franz Hildebrandt and Oliver A. Beckerlegge, with the assistance of James Dale (Nashville: Abingdon, 1983). Begun as *The Oxford Edition of the Works of John Wesley* by Oxford University Press (1975–1983), this critical edition of Wesley's *Works* was continued as *The Bicentennial Edition of the Works of John Wesley* by Abingdon Press, 1984– .

2. For the rationale for hymn and text see the afterword at the end of this introduction and chapter 5.

3. The terms *itinerancy* and *itineracy* are used interchangeably in United Methodism. I prefer and use the former.

4. *The Book of Discipline of The United Methodist Church—2004* (Nashville: The United Methodist Publishing House, 2004), 242-43; hereinafter *Discipline*/UMC 2004. (Unless otherwise noted, paragraph notations will be to this *Discipline*.)

5. Actions regarding extension ministries taken by the 2008 General Conference, shortly before this book went to press, will no doubt add additional questions. On the deacon, see Rosemary Skinner Keller, Gerald F. Moede, and Mary Elizabeth Moore, *Called to Serve: The United Methodist Diaconate* (Nashville: Division of Diaconal Ministry of the General Board of Higher Education and Ministry, 1987); and John E. Harnish, *The Orders of Ministry in The United Methodist Church* (Nashville: Abingdon, 2000).

6. Statistics courtesy of the General Council on Finance and Administration.

7. See Russell E. Richey, *Marks of Methodism: Theology in Ecclesial Practice* (Nashville: Abingdon, 2005).

Chapter 1: Connectional Tasks and Accountability

1. *The Works of John Wesley 7, A Collection of Hymns for the Use of the People Called Methodists,* 690-91, #501; *The Methodist Hymn-Book,* 578, #688.

2. By 1844 the *Discipline* had aggregated these several roles in specifying exceptions to the two-year rule for appointments. In answer to a question about the duties of a bishop, the *Discipline* (MEC 1844, 26-27) stated:

   > *Answ.* 1. To preside in our conferences. To fix the appointments of the preachers for the several circuits, provided he shall not allow any preacher to remain in the same station more than two years successively; except the presiding elders, the general editor, the general book steward and his assistant, the editor and assistant editor of the Christian Advocate and Journal, the editor of the Sunday school books, the corresponding secretaries, editors and agents at Cincinnati, the supernumerary, superannuated and worn-out preachers, missionaries among the Indians, missionaries to our people of colour and on foreign stations, chaplains to state prison and military posts, those preachers that may be appointed to labour for the special benefit of seamen, the preacher or preachers that may be stationed in the city of New-Orleans, and the presidents, principals, or teachers of seminaries of learning, which are or may be under our superintendence; and also, when requested by an annual conference, to appoint a preacher for a longer time than two years to any seminary of learning not under our care. . . . He shall have authority, when requested by an annual conference, to appoint an agent, whose duty it shall be to travel throughout the bounds of such conference, for the purpose of establishing and aiding sabbath schools, and distributing tracts, and also to appoint an agent or agents for the benefit of our literary institutions.

3. *Minutes of the Methodist Conferences, Annually Held in America; From 1773 to 1813, Inclusive* (New York: Daniel Hitt and Thomas Ware, 1813), 1789, 82; 1790, 93; 1791, 104; 1792, 116; 1793, 129; 1794, 144; 1795, 156-62; 1797, 195, 198-99; 1798, 211; 1799, 226; 1801, 259. For some reason, in the intervening year the *Minutes* reverted to the earlier form.

4. On the evolution of the office and especially the role of John Dickins, designated publisher in or around 1783, see James P. Pilkington, *The Methodist Publishing House* (Nashville: Abingdon, 1968), 1:43-116.

5. *Minutes*, 1802, 278. For similar earlier treatment see *Minutes*, 1789, 82-83; 1790, 93; 1791, 104; 1792, 113, 116; 1793, 129; 1794, 144; 1795, 157-62; 1796, 182; 1797, 194, 196.

6. *Minutes*, 1803, 297, 300.

7. *Minutes*, 1804, 322.

8. *Minutes*, 1809, 454-55, 458, 459, 460.

9. Minutes, 1809, 459.

10. Russell E. Richey, Kenneth E. Rowe, Jean Miller Schmidt, *The Methodist Experience in America* (Nashville: Abingdon, 2000), 2:56-67. Hereinafter abbreviated *MEA*.

11. Pilkington, *Methodist Publishing House*, 1:43-116; *The Journal and Letters of Francis Asbury*, ed. Elmer T. Clark, 3 vols. (London: Epworth; Nashville: Abingdon, 1958). Hereinafter Asbury's works are referenced as *JLFA*. See indexes of the former for Asbury entries, and the indexes in volume 3 of the latter for Dickins entries.

12. *Proceedings of the Bishop and Presiding Elders of the Methodist-Episcopal Church, in Council Assembled, at Baltimore, on the First Day of December, 1789* (Baltimore: William Woodard and James Angell, 1789), 3-7; *Minutes, Taken at a Council of the Bishop and Delegated Elders of the Methodist-Episcopal Church: Held at Baltimore in the State of Maryland, December 1, 1790* (Baltimore: W. Goddard and J. Angell, 1790), 3-8.

13. *Minutes, Taken at a Council of Bishops and Delegated Elders of the Methodist Episcopal Church; Held at Baltimore in the State of Maryland, December 1, 1790* (Baltimore: W. Goodard and J. Angell, 1790), 3-8.

14. *JGC*/MEC, 1796, 17.

15. *Minutes*, 1797, 198-99.

16. "Journal of a Conference Held in New York, Tuesday 12th June 1804" (Typescript, Drew University), 22/52.

17. On the development of the office of chaplain, see chapter 4.

18. *Minutes of . . . the Philadelphia Conference of the Methodist Episcopal Church*, 1862, 36-41.

19. *Minutes of the . . . Philadelphia Conference of the Methodist Episcopal Church*, 1865.

20. *Minutes of the Annual Conferences of the Methodist Episcopal Church*, 1862, 64-66.

21. Abel Stevens, *Memorials of the Early Progress of Methodism in the Eastern States*, 2nd Series (New York: Carlton & Phillips, 1854), 39.

22. *Minutes of the New England Conference of the Methodist Episcopal Church . . . 1868*, 8-9; *Minutes of the New England Conference of the Methodist Episcopal Church . . . 1872*, 5, 6.

23. William F. Warren, "Ministerial Education in Our Church," *Methodist Quarterly Review* 54 (April 1872): 246-67, 260. Emphasis added.

Chapter 2: Extension Ministers: Connectional Builders

1. *The Works of John Wesley 7, A Collection of Hymns for the Use of the People Called Methodists*, 100-102, #17.
2. John McClintock, "Rev. Nathan Bangs, D.D.," *The Ladies' Repository* 19 (1859): 321-24. McClintock—teacher, editor, pastor, first president of Drew Theological Seminary—is perhaps best remembered today as the joint author with James Strong of the twelve-volume *Cyclopaedia of Biblical, Theological and Ecclesiastical Literature* (1883–87).
3. Bangs, *History*, 2:390-418. Bangs covers the errors on pp. 413-17.
4. For a very different take on Bangs's agenda, see Roger Finke and Rodney Stark, *The Churching of America* (New Brunswick, N.J.: Rutgers University Press, 1992), 145-69; and John H. Wigger, *Taking Heaven by Storm: Methodism and the Rise of Popular Christianity in America* (New York: Oxford University Press, 1998), 189-90.
5. On Bangs's life and work, see Richard Everett Hermann, "Nathan Bangs: Apologist for American Methodism" (PhD diss., Emory University, 1973).
6. "Journals of the New York Annual Conference, 1800–1839," transcribed by William R. Phinney, 3 vols. Drew University Library. Notations refer to year and x/y denoting page numbers in manuscript (x) and typescript (y), in this instance 1802: 12/42.
7. The best access to his multiple roles is by scrutiny of the typescript at Drew University of the *Journals of the New York Conference*, from 1800 on.
8. *Journals of the New York Conference from 1821 to 1829*, 1827, 98, 101, 102, 111, 112, 117. *Journals of the New York Conference from 1821 to 1829*, 1828, 120, 121, 122, 127-28, 137, 140.
9. For listing of MEC, MECS, and MC book agents and editors, see *EWM*, 2:2709-11.
10. Candy Gunther Brown, *Word in the World: Evangelical Writing, Publishing, and Reading in America, 1789–1880* (Chapel Hill: The University of North Carolina Press, 2004), 9-13, 46.
11. The aforementioned listing (*EWM*) identifies the book agents, *Advocate* and *Review* heads, and editors of Sunday school publications who were subsequently elected bishop.

12. *The Errors of Hopkinsianism Detected and Refuted* (New York: D. Nitt and T. Ware, 1815); *The Reformer Reformed: or A Second Part of the Errors of Hopkinsianism Detected and Refuted* (New York: John C. Totten, 1816); *An Examination of the Doctrine of Predestination* (New York: J. C. Totten, 1817); *A Vindication of Methodist Episcopacy* (New York: W. A. Mercein, 1820).

13. See Thomas A. Langford, *Practical Divinity: Theology in the Wesleyan Tradition* (Nashville: Abingdon, 1983), 78-86.

14. For committee reports on Bangs's manuscript in 1815 and book in 1818, see *Journals of the New York Conference from 1800 to 1820*, 1815: 99-100/129-30 and 1818: 138/168.

15. *JGC*/MEC 1816, 1:155.

16. Pilkington/Vernon, *Methodist Publishing House*, 1:172, 169, 117.

17. Brown, *Word in the World*, 155.

18. "Constitution adopted April 2, 1827, Sunday School Union of the Methodist Episcopal Church," *MQR* 10/8 (Aug. 1827): 367.

19. *JGC*/MEC 1824, 295; *Discipline*/MEC 1824, 58; *Discipline*/MEC 1828, 58.

20. "Circular address, and Constitution of the Missionary and Bible Society, of the Methodist Episcopal Church in America," *MQR*/MEC (June 1819): 277-79. (Note: The name of the society was subsequently simplified to Missionary Society.)

21. Samuel Luttrell Akers, *The First Hundred Years of Wesleyan College, 1836–1936* (Macon, Ga.: Wesleyan College, 1976). The *Handbook of United Methodist-Related Schools, Colleges, Universities and Theological Schools* notes that "Greensboro College . . . was chartered by the Methodist Church in 1838 as a women's college." See *Handbook of United Methodist-Related Schools, Colleges, Universities and Theological Schools* (Nashville: General Board of Higher Education and Ministry, The United Methodist Church, 1996), 89.

22. Donald G. Tewksbury, *The Founding of American Colleges and Universities Before the Civil War* (New York: Arno Press & The New York Times, 1969), 103-11. By contrast, Tewksbury estimates that the Presbyterians founded forty-nine (102).

23. For further information on Durbin, see the entry in *The Methodists* by James E. Kirby, Russell E. Richey, and Kenneth E. Rowe (Westport, Conn.: Greenwood Press, 1996), 291-92; see also the estimates of him by John A. Roche, *The Life of John Price Durbin* (New York: Phillips and Hunt, 1889) and "John Price Durbin," *MQR*/MEC 69 (May 1887): 329-54.

24. *Minutes of the Philadelphia Conference of the Methodist Episcopal Church*, 1835

(typescript version of apparently printed minutes), 10. On his presidency, see James Henry Morgan, *Dickinson College: The History of One Hundred Fifty Years, 1783–1933* (Carlisle, Pa.: Dickinson College, 1933); and Charles Coleman Sellers, *Dickinson College: A History* (Middletown, Conn.: Wesleyan University Press, 1973).

25. J. P. Durbin was, for instance, listed first as delegate to the 1844 General Conference. *Minutes of the Philadelphia Conference of the Methodist Episcopal Church*, 1844, 10.

26. *Minutes of the Philadelphia Conference of the Methodist Episcopal Church*, 1845, 12.

27. *Minutes of the Philadelphia Conference of the Methodist Episcopal Church*, 1846, 14.

28. *Minutes of the Philadelphia Conference of the Methodist Episcopal Church*, 1849, 5. This office is now known as the district superintendent. By that time the *Minutes* listed a North German Mission in N. Philadelphia District and South German Mission in S. Philadelphia District; see *Minutes of the Philadelphia Conference of the Methodist Episcopal Church*, 1849, 5-6.

29. Francis H. Tees et al., *Pioneering in Penn's Woods. Philadelphia Methodist Episcopal Annual Conference Through One Hundred Fifty Years* (n.p.: The Philadelphia Conference Tract Society of the Methodist Episcopal Church, 1937), 117-19.

30. Morgan, *Dickinson College*, 248-72, 283-94; Sellers, *Dickinson College*, 195-229.

31. Ibid., 117-19; J. M. Reid, *Missions and Missionary Society of the Methodist Episcopal Church*, 2 vols. (New York: Phillips & Hunt, 1879), 1:32-39. See also the revised and extended edition with J. T. Gracey, 3 vols. (New York: Eaton & Mains, 1895, 1896); Wade Crawford Barclay, *History of Methodist Missions*, 3 vols. (New York: Board of Missions and Church Extension of the Methodist Church, 1949-); Dana L. Robert, *American Women in Mission: A Social History of Their Thought and Practice* (Macon, Ga: Mercer University Press, 1996).

32. *Minutes of the Philadelphia Conference of the Methodist Episcopal Church*, 1850, 6.

33. *Minutes of the Troy Conference*, 1851, 21-22.

34. "Minutes Erie Conference for the Year 1850," *Minutes of the First Twenty Sessions of the Erie Annual Conference* (Published by Order of the Conference, 1907), 257.

35. For Erie see *Minutes*, 257. Compare *Minutes of the Maine Annual Conference*, 1850, 10-11; and *Minutes of the New England Annual Conference*, 1851, 30-31.

36. *Minutes of the Philadelphia Conference of the Methodist Episcopal Church*, 1851, 12.

37. Ibid., 8.

38. *Annual Report of the Missionary Society of the Methodist Episcopal Church*, 1854, 9. As an interim step, the General Conference of 1844 had empowered the bishops to take such action. *The General Conferences of the Methodist Episcopal Church From 1792 to 1896*, ed. Lewis Curts (Cincinnati: Curts & Jennings; New York; Eaton & Mains, 1900), 367-68.

39. *Annual Report of the Missionary Society of the Methodist Episcopal Church*, 1854, 33.

40. *Minutes of the Philadelphia Conference of the Methodist Episcopal Church*, 1856, 14, 1. At this point Philadelphia created thirteen standing committees. Missions was third on the list, being preceded by Public Worship and Necessitous Cases. To the latter, incidentally, the conference stewards were appropriately appointed.

41. *Minutes of the Annual Conferences of the Methodist Episcopal Church*, 1859, 1. The preceding year it had begun to include tables, one of "Appointments of Preachers, With Their Post Office Address," another listing names of all preachers by year of admission to the conference, with 1806 being the first. *Minutes of the Philadelphia Conference of the Methodist Episcopal Church*, 1858, 9-12, 19-20. By 1859, Philadelphia added a very interesting "Plan of Statistics for Annual Minutes" to those two items.

42. *Minutes of the Philadelphia Conference of the Methodist Episcopal Church*, 1862, 13.

43. *Minutes of the Eightieth Session of the Philadelphia Conference of the Methodist Episcopal Church*, 1867. The minutes also include "Forty-Sixth Annual Report of the Missionary Society of the Methodist Episcopal Church, within the Bounds of the Philadelphia Conference, for Promoting Domestic and Foreign Missions," 65-116.

44. Ibid., 6-7.

45. Ibid., 65.

46. Ibid., 10, 47.

47. Ibid., 10.

48. *Minutes of the Philadelphia Conference of the Methodist Episcopal Church*, 1868, 12.

Chapter 3: Chaplains

1. *The Works of John Wesley* 7, *A Collection of Hymns for the Use of the People Called Methodists*, 399-400, #258, Part 1 of 3 on Ephesians 6.

2. Methodists related to the Revolution in a spectrum of stances. One or two were actually collaborators. A number as loyalists departed for England or Canada. Many, like Lee, were pacifists. Some, like Garrettson, were persecuted for such

a stance. And many others, including some preachers, signed on to the patriot military cause. On these several roles, see Dee E. Andrews, *The Methodists and Revolutionary America, 1760–1800: The Shaping of an Evangelical Culture* (Princeton, N.J.: Princeton University Press, 2000).

3. Minton Thrift, *Memoir of the Rev. Jesse Lee. With Extracts from His Journals* (New York: N. Bangs and T. Mason for the Methodist Episcopal Church, 1823), 26-33.

4. John W. Brinsfield, "The Chaplains of the Confederacy," in *Faith in the Fight: Civil War Chaplains*, ed. John W. Brinsfield et al. (Mechanicsburg, Pa.: Stackpole Books, 2003), 54-55; John W. Brinsfield, comp. and ed., *The Spirit Divided: Memoirs of Civil War Chaplains: The Confederacy* (Macon, Ga.: Mercer University Press, 2006).

5. The listing was in answer to a Disciplinary question concerning the episcopacy and appointments. See *Discipline*/MEC 1844, 26-27.

> *Quest.* 3. What are the duties of a bishop.
>
> *Answ.* 1. To preside in our conferences. 2. To fix the appointments of the preachers for the several circuits, provided he shall not allow any preacher to remain in the same station more than two years successively; except the presiding elders, the general editor, the general book steward and his assistant, the editor and assistant editor of the Christian Advocate and Journal, the editor of the Sunday school books, the corresponding secretaries, editors and agents at Cincinnati, the supernumerary, superannuated and worn-out preachers, missionaries among the Indians, missionaries to our people of colour and on foreign stations, chaplains to state prison and military posts, those preachers that may be appointed to labour for the special benefit of seamen, the preacher or preachers that may be stationed in the city of New-Orleans, and the presidents, principals, or teachers of seminaries of learning, which are or may be under our superintendence; and also, when requested by an annual conference, to appoint a preacher for a longer time than two years to any seminary of learning not under our care . . . He shall have authority, when requested by an annual conference, to appoint an agent, whose duty it shall be to travel throughout the bounds of such conference, for the purpose of establishing and aiding sabbath schools, and distributing tracts, and also to appoint an agent or agents for the benefit of our literary institutions.

6. For the citation, the episcopal counsel, and the complexities of attitudes toward slavery and secession, see Christopher H. Owen, *The Sacred Flame of Love: Methodism and Society in Nineteenth-Century Georgia* (Athens: University of Georgia Press, 1998), especially 104-6, 93-95; also Beth Barton Schweiger, *The Gospel Working Up: Progress and the Pulpit in Nineteenth-Century Virginia* (New York and Oxford: Oxford University Press, 2000), 93-95. On the spirituality of the church, see Mitchell Snay, *Gospel of Disunion: Religion and Separatism in the Antebellum South* (Cambridge: Cambridge University Press, 1993; Chapel Hill: University of North Carolina Press, 1997), 151-80.

7. Brinsfield, "The Chaplains of the Confederacy," *Faith in the Fight*, 51-92.

8. Brinsfield, *Spirit Divided*, 7, 10. From the full members of conference, the MECS bishops appointed 318 of the Methodist chaplains and permitted 109 to serve in other capacities (96). See also Brinsfield, "The Chaplains of the Confederacy," *Faith in the Fight*, 61; Gardiner H. Shattuck, *A Shield and Hiding Place* (Macon, Ga.: Mercer University Press, 1987), 51-72.

9. Sledge, *"Five Dollars and Myself,"* 85-109; Brinsfield, *Spirit Divided*, 140-42, 183-93; Steven E. Woodworth, *While God Is Marching On: The Religious World of Civil War Soldiers* (Lawrence: University Press of Kansas, 2001), 160-63.

10. Brinsfield, "The Chaplains of the Confederacy," *Faith in the Fight*, 55-58, 71-72.

11. Schweiger, *Gospel Working Up*, 99-100, 107; Brinsfield, "The Chaplains of the Confederacy," *Faith in the Fight*, 81-82, 84-85.

12. William W. Bennett, *A Narrative of the Great Revival in the Southern Armies During the Late Civil War Between the States of the Federal Union* (Philadelphia: Claxton, Remsen & Haffelfinger, 1877).

13. Schweiger, *Gospel Working Up*, 101-2.

14. Brinsfield, *Spirit Divided*, 185-86.

15. Ibid., 191.

16. James W. May, "The War Years," *History of American Methodism*, ed. Emory S. Bucke et al. (New York: Abingdon, 1964), 2:211-14.

17. Kenneth Brown and P. Lewis Brevard, *History of the Churches of Christ in Christian Union* (Circleville, Ohio: Circle Press, 1980), 28.

18. George R. Crooks, *The Life of Bishop Matthew Simpson of the Methodist Episcopal Church* (New York: Harper & Brothers, 1891), 366-406.

19. *Minutes of the . . . Philadelphia Conference of the Methodist Episcopal Church*, 1862, 7, 45-46.

20. *Minutes of the . . . Philadelphia Conference of the Methodist Episcopal Church*, 1864, 15, 44-45, 48, 49.

21. *Minutes of the Sixth Session of the Newark Conference*, 1863, 16-20, 32-33.

22. *Proceedings of the Sixth Annual Meeting of the National Association of Local Preachers of the Methodist Episcopal Church . . . Union M. E. Church, Philadelphia . . . October 10-12, 1863. Together with An Appendix, Containing the Annual Sermon and the Constitution of the Association* (Pittsburgh, 1863), 14.

23. *JGC*/MEC 1864, 281-91.

24. "Report No. III of the Committee on the State of the Country," *JGC*/MEC 1864, 380-83; Moorhead, *American Apocalypse*, 141-42.

25. A. W. Drury, *History of the Church of the United Brethren in Christ* (Dayton: United Brethren Publishing House, 1931), 456.

26. Edward J. Drinkhouse, *History of Methodist Reform* (Baltimore: Board of Publication of the Methodist Protestant Church, 1899), 2:452-55.

27. William Warren Sweet, *The Methodist Episcopal Church and the Civil War* (Cincinnati: Methodist Book Concern Press, 1912), 93-95.

28. Woodworth, *While God Is Marching On*, 94.

29. May, "The War Years," 226-28.

30. Benedict Maryniak, "Union Military Chaplains," in *Faith in the Fight*, 3-49, 45.

31. Maryniak, ibid., 9-12, quotation from 12; Brinsfield, "The Chaplains of the Confederacy," *Faith in the Fight*, 55; Shattuck, *A Shield and Hiding Place*, 51-72.

32. Long, *Revival of 1857-58* (New York: Oxford University Press, 1998), 87-91, 117-20; Maryniak, "Union Military Chaplains," 20-21, 28-31; Woodworth, *While God Is Marching On*, 167-74; Shattuck, *A Shield and Hiding Place*, 24-33, 81-92.

33. Lemuel Moss, *Annals of the United States Christian Commission* (Philadelphia: J. B. Lippincott & Co., 1868), 106-8, 110-13, 131; May, "The War Years," 222-25.

34. Shattuck, *A Shield and Hiding Place*, 89-92, quotation from 89.

35. *Discipline*/UMC 2004, 594, ¶1421.5(a). The whole of ¶1421, pp. 590-96, applies.

36. *Discipline*/MEC 1844, 26-27.

Chapter 4: Connecting: An Extension Task

1. A version of this chapter appears as the introduction to *Connectionalism: Ecclesiology, Mission, and Identity*, ed. Russell E. Richey, Dennis M. Campbell, and William B. Lawrence, vol. 1 (Nashville: Abingdon, 1997). Adapted by permission. A fuller set of notes may be found there.

2. *The Works of John Wesley* 7; *A Collection of Hymns for the Use of the People Called Methodists*, 344, #211.

3. I have addressed this topic several times, most recently in *Marks of Methodism*, as well as in the aforementioned *Connectionalism*.

4. See Donald T. Kauffman, *The Dictionary of Religious Terms* (Westwood, N.J.: Fleming H. Revell, 1967).

5. Certainly one important exception is the United Church of Christ, which, on its Puritan or Congregational side, combined elements of the Radical and Magisterial Reformations in complex fashion. American Puritanism sought to be both congregational and established. Until well after the Revolution, the Congregational churches were established in New England.

6. One would need to concede that these distinctions are handy and somewhat arbitrary. No church now behaves in a more centralized, coercive, connectional way than the Southern Baptist Convention. And all connectional churches have had to come to terms with localism and a congregationalist mentality, particularly within the flock.

7. The connectional background for the Evangelical and United Brethren traditions is more complex. While showing some indebtedness to Wesley, it has deeper roots in the Magisterial Reformation (Lutheran and Reformed, respectively), but betrays as well the critiques mounted by Pietism and Anabaptism.

8. A different statement of the argument of this paragraph can be found in Russell E. Richey, "The Legacy of Francis Asbury: The Teaching Office in Episcopal Methodism," *Quarterly Review* 15/2 (Summer 1995): 145-74. The section as a whole depends on Russell E. Richey, *The Methodist Conference in America: A History* (Nashville: Kingswood, 1996); and Russell E. Richey, *Early American Methodism* (Bloomington and Indianapolis: Indiana University Press, 1991).

9. For the levels of dependence upon and independence from the Methodist Episcopal pattern in the United Brethren and Evangelical Association, see J. Bruce Behney and Paul H. Eller, *The History of the Evangelical United Brethren Church*, ed. Kenneth W. Krueger (Nashville: Abingdon, 1979).

10. Minton Thrift, *Memoir of the Rev. Jesse Lee. With Extracts from His Journals* (New York: N. Bangs and T. Mason for the Methodist Episcopal Church, 1823), 48-60. From the itinerant's angle, his own "liberty" keyed the process. Hence the constant assessment of whether the word was preached and heard:

> "Sunday 7th of March, I preached at Robert Jones', to a serious congregation, and blessed be God, it was a happy time, and the Lord was among us of a truth."
>
> "I continued to preach with much liberty. . . ."

"Sunday 4th, I preached at Robert Jones', to a serious company of people, and had liberty among them..." (59-60).

[June] "Sunday 20th, I preached at Coles, but the congregation was so large, that the house would not hold them, of course we had to look for another place; we got under the shade of some trees, where I spoke with great freedom, and with a heart drawn out in love to the souls of the people; and I felt a longing desire to be instrumental in bringing their souls to God. When I met the class, the friends wept greatly, while they heard each other tell of the goodness of God to their souls" (66-67).

11. The second edition of the *Discipline* printed with *The Sunday Service of the Methodists in North America* (n.p.: London, 1786), ran to twenty-nine pages.

12. William Johnson Everett and Thomas Edward Frank, "Constitutional Order in United Methodism and American Culture," in *Connectionalism*, 41-73.

13. See the extended discussion and documentation in *Early American Methodism*.

14. "Minutes for 1780," in *Minutes of the Methodist Conferences, Annually Held in America; From 1773 to 1813, Inclusive*, 26.

15. John Ffirth, *The Experience and Gospel Labours of the Rev. Benjamin Abbott*. Published by Ezekiel Cooper (Philadelphia: Solomon W. Conrad, 1802), 164-66.

16. *Extracts of the Journals of the Rev. Dr. Coke's Five Visits to America* (London: Printed by G. Paramore, 1784), 35-36.

17. Thomas Coke and Francis Asbury, *The Doctrines and Disciplines of the Methodist Episcopal Church, in America* (Philadelphia: Henry Tuckniss, 1798), 38-53, 146-48. Excerpts reproduced in *The Methodist Experience in America*, ed. Russell E. Richey, Kenneth E. Rowe, and Jean Miller Schmidt, 2 vols. (Nashville: Abingdon, 2000), 2:128-31, quotation from 131.

18. *Autobiography of Peter Cartwright, the Backwoods Preacher*, ed. William Peter Strickland (New York: The Methodist Book Concern, [1856?]; reprinted and edited by Charles L. Wallis (Nashville: Abingdon, 1956); and *Fifty Years as a Presiding Elder*, ed. W. S. Hooper (Cincinnati: Walden and Stowe, 1871; New York: Phillips and Hunt, 1871).

19. Fred W. Price, "The Role of the Presiding Elder in the Growth of the Methodist Episcopal Church, 1784–1832," PhD diss., Drew University, 1987.

20. George Peck, ed., *Sketches and Incidents; or A Budget from the Saddle-Bags of a Superannuated Itinerant* (New York: G. Lane and P. P. Sandford for the

MEC, 1844-45; reprinted Salem, Ohio: Schmul Publishing, 1988. Attrib. to Abel Stevens), 101. Compare another retrospective, also reported by Peck:

> His quarterly meeting was on Lycoming circuit. It was held in a barn, and the meeting was highly favored of the Lord. In those days there was seldom a quarterly meeting held where there were not souls converted. The Methodists would attend from every part of the circuit. Twenty, or thirty, and even fifty miles was not so far off but they would make an effort to attend, and look upon it as a great privilege to go to quarterly meeting. They would come on horseback through the woods, and from the settlements and towns in their great old-fashioned wagons, drawn by oxen very often, and crowded full; sometimes they would come down the river in canoes. They came with hearts alive to God, and every one was ambitious of excelling in getting nearest to, and in doing most for God and truth.
>
> Consequently many sinners were converted before the meeting closed. Such exhortations and prayers, such shouting, for old-fashioned Methodists would shout. Their thorough enjoyment, their genuine tokens of holy delight, their ready responses, always expressed in a hearty manner, bore the preacher onward to success. To preach tamely before such an audience would be an impossibility. No Christian could slumber in such a vivifying atmosphere, no aspirations became weary, no ardor grew cold. (George Peck, *Early Methodism Within the Bounds of the Old Genesee Conference from 1788 to 1828* [New York: Carlton & Porter, 1860], 419-20).

This account was for a quarterly meeting in 1814 at Painted Post, on the northern Pennsylvania border, for George Harmon, presiding elder on the Susquehanna District, and was rendered by his daughter.

21. *Discipline*/UMC 2004, 243-44, ¶344.1, ¶344.1.*a*.1.
22. The representative, delegative, republican, political style of connection might well be introduced and developed here. It clearly has early origins—indeed, roots—in typically American patterns of political behavior that Methodists began drawing into their religious life from the 1760s onward. I choose to focus on this style of conference as expressed not in this early "republican" stage or during the formative phases of the Methodist Protestant movement but in the twentieth century. To be sure, a good case can be made for introducing at this point what Frank and Everett term the "federal" style.

23. Nathan Bangs, *An Original Church of Christ: Or, A Scriptural Vindication of the Orders and Powers of the Ministry of the Methodist Episcopal Church*. Published by T. Mason and G. Lane. (New York: J. Collord, 1837), 348-51. Bangs continues:

    > This is a general outline of the system, the different parts of which have grown out of the exigencies of the times, suiting itself to the mental, moral, and spiritual wants of men, and expanding itself so as to embrace the largest possible number of individuals as objects of its benevolence. I may well be suspected of partiality to a system, to the benign operation of which I am so much indebted, and which has exerted such a beneficial influence upon the best interests of mankind; but I cannot avoid thinking that I see in it that "perfection of beauty, out of which God hath shined," and that emanation of divine truth and light, which is destined, unless it should unhappily degenerate from its primitive beauty and simplicity "into a plant of a strange vine," and thus lose its original energy of character, to do its full share in enlightening and converting the world.

24. A. J. Kynett, "'Report of the Board of Church Extension' after the change to the General Conference of 1876," *JGC*/MEC 1876, 602-4.
25. "Report of Committee on Benevolent Societies," *JGC*/MEC 1872, 295-98.
26. Everett and Frank, "Constitutional Order in United Methodism and American Culture," *Connectionalism*, 41-73.
27. Jean Miller Schmidt, *Grace Sufficient: A History of Women in American Methodism, 1760-1939* (Nashville: Abingdon, 1999), 213-31.
28. Concern to make Methodist polity behave according to American precept had begun when the first conferences convened. It had been made operative by Asbury's call for a general conference and elective episcopacy and found expression in the 1808 constitution and provision for delegated representation. It had animated the reform efforts of African Methodists, Republicans, Methodist Protestants, Wesleyans, Free Methodists, and Nazarenes. It had encouraged women and blacks in their quest for representation, ordination, and episcopal orders. Yet, while Methodists accommodated themselves to American political practice over the course of their history, only in 1939 did they accord American civil theory full Disciplinary status. The reunion of 1939 made federalism, political rights, representation, and separation of powers into Methodist principle. The linchpin in this federalism was the jurisdictional conference, an accommodation to Methodist racism and (Southern) regionalism.

29. See *Discipline*/MC 1940, 350-51, for stipulations for staffing of the Board of Education and elsewhere for other boards.

30. Judge Nathan Newby (Pacific Annual Conference), *The Daily Christian Advocate*/MEC 1939, 181, 183-84.

31. *The Daily Christian Advocate*/MEC 1939, 179, 181, 182.

32. See Richey, *Methodist Conference in America*, 145-74.

33. Sarah Sloan Kreutziger, "Wesley's Legacy of Social Holiness: The Methodist Settlement Movement and American Social Reform," in *Connectionalism*, 137-75.

34. Robert C. Monk, "United Methodist Campus Ministry and the Methodist Student Movement," in *Connectionalism*, 179-202.

35. Bradley J. Longfield, "Methodist Identities and the Founding of Methodist Universities," in *Connectionalism*, 95-113.

36. Monk, "United Methodist Campus Ministry and the Methodist Student Movement," in *Connectionalism*, 179-202.

37. For a discussion of changes in denominational life, see Milton J. Coalter, John M. Mulder, and Louis B. Weeks, *The Re-forming Tradition: Presbyterians and Mainstream Protestantism* (Louisville: Westminster/John Knox, 1992); and Robert Bruce Mullin and Russell E. Richey, ed., *Reimagining Denomination-alism: Interpretive Essays* (New York and Oxford: Oxford University Press, 1994), especially my chapter, "Denominations and Denominationalism: An American Morphology."

38. It is now an autonomous Methodist Church in affiliated relationship with The United Methodist Church.

39. Grant S. Shockley, ed., *Heritage and Hope: The African-American Presence in United Methodism* (Nashville: Abingdon, 1991, esp. 209-10, 225-28; William B. McClain, *Black People in the Methodist Church* (Cambridge: Schenkman Publishing, 1984); James S. Thomas, *Methodism's Racial Dilemma: The Story of the Central Jurisdiction* (Nashville: Abingdon, 1992).

40. Homer Noley, *First White Frost: Native Americans and United Methodism* (Nashville: Abingdon, 1991), 225-30.

41. Justo L. Gonzalez, ed., *Each in Our Own Tongue: A History of Hispanic United Methodism* (Nashville: Abingdon, 1991), 60-61, 155-59.

42. Artemio R. Guillermo, ed., *Churches Aflame: Asian Americans and United Methodism* (Nashville: Abingdon, 1991), 135-53.

43. The term "struggle" and the recognition of the formation of these groups as a prevalent pattern in late twentieth-century denominations belong to Robert

Wuthnow. See his *The Restructuring of American Religion: Society and Faith Since World War II* (Princeton, N.J.: Princeton University Press, 1988); *The Struggle for America's Soul: Evangelicals, Liberals, and Secularism* (Grand Rapids, Mich.: Eerdmans, 1989); and *Christianity in the Twenty-first Century: Reflections on the Challenges Ahead* (New York: Oxford University Press, 1993). See also my essay in *Reimagining Denominationalism.*

44. *Discipline/*UMC 1996, 114.

45. *Discipline/*UMC 2004, 87; *Discipline/*UMC 1996, 114; see Thomas Edward Frank, *Polity, Practice, and the Mission of The United Methodist Church*, updated edition (Nashville: Abingdon, 2006), 162-63, 173-94.

46. *JGC/*MEC 1928, 152-74.

47. *JGC/*MEC, 1920, 1457, 424-25. The action amended Division III, Chapter, I, Article II, ¶35 to read, "A Local Conference shall be organized in each Pastoral Charge, and be composed of such persons and have such powers as the General Conference may direct." In the floor action and debate, the original language of the legislation, which had spoken of "Church conference," was so amended.

48. *JGC/*MC 1940, 236-38.

49. See *Discipline/*UMC 2004, ¶331.

50. On the congregationalizing of itinerancy and connection, see "Are the Local Church and Denominational Bureaucracy Twins?" in *Questions for the Twenty-First Century Church*, ed. Russell E. Richey, Dennis M. Campbell, and William B. Lawrence. United Methodist and American Culture Series 4 (Nashville: Abingdon, 1999), 232-41.

51. This is question 1 of The Shorter Catechism. The Westminster Larger Catechism differed slightly: "Question 1 'What is the chief and highest end of man? Answer: Man's chief and highest end is to glorify God, and fully to enjoy him forever.'"

52. *Discipline/*MEC 1787, 3-7.

Chapter 5: Thinking About Thinking About Extension Ministry

1. *The Works of John Wesley 7, A Collection of Hymns for the Use of the People Called Methodists*, 472, #317.

2. On the quadrilateral, see Ted A. Campbell, "The 'Wesleyan Quadrilateral': The Story of a Modern Methodist Myth," and Albert C. Outler, "The Wesleyan Quadrilateral—In John Wesley," in *Doctrine and Theology in The United Methodist Church*, ed. Thomas A. Langford (Nashville: Kingswood, 1991),

154-61 and 75-88; W. Stephen Gunter, et al., *Wesley and the Quadrilateral: Renewing the Conversation* (Nashville: Abingdon, 1997); Scott J. Jones, *John Wesley's Conception and Use of Scripture* (Nashville: Kingswood, 1995); Scott J. Jones, *United Methodist Doctrine: The Extreme Center* (Nashville: Abingdon, 2002); and Walter Klaiber and Manfred Marquardt, *Living Grace: An Outline of United Methodist Theology*, translated and adapted by J. Steven O'Malley and Ulrike R. M. Guthrie (Nashville: Abingdon, 2001), 17-92.

3. See *Baptism, Eucharist and Ministry (BEM)*, Faith and Order Paper No. 111 (Geneva: World Council of Churches, 1982), 26. Available online at http://www.wcc-coe.org/wcc/what/faith/bem1.html.

Epilogue: A Word to Extension Ministers

1. *The Works of John Wesley 7, A Collection of Hymns for the Use of the People Called Methodists*, 699-700, #508. It is the fourth of four love feast hymns.

2. *The Methodist Hymn-Book*, 623, #752. It does not appear in *The Works of John Wesley 7*.

3. *The Works of John Wesley 7*, 699. This is the second verse of the hymn cited in the beginning of this chapter.

4. *The Works of John Wesley 7*, 382-83, #241.

5. *The Works of John Wesley 7*, 194-95, #92, following the title and part of the section titled "Describing Inward Religion."

For Further Reading

Andrews. Dee E. *The Methodists and Revolutionary America, 1760–1800: The Shaping of an Evangelical Culture*. Princeton, N.J.: Princeton University Press, 2000.

Brinsfield, John Wesley, Jr. *The Spirit Divided: Memoirs of Civil War Chaplains: The Confederacy*. Macon, Ga.: Mercer University Press, 2006.

Crain, Margaret Ann. *The Promise of the United Methodist Order of Deacon in the Twenty-first Century: Partners with the Whole People of God* (Monograph). Nashville: General Board of Higher Education and Ministry, The United Methodist Church, 2007.

Crain, Margaret Ann, and Jack L. Seymour, with Jimmy Carr and Joaquín García. *A Deacon's Heart: The New United Methodist Diaconate*. Nashville: Abingdon, 2001.

Frank, Thomas Edward. *Polity, Practice, and the Mission of The United Methodist Church*, updated edition. Nashville: Abingdon, 2006.

Guillermo, Artemio R., ed. *Churches Aflame: Asian Americans and United Methodism*. Nashville: Abingdon, 1991.

Harnish, John E. *The Orders of Ministry in The United Methodist Church*. Nashville: Abingdon, 2000.

Holifield, E. Brooks. *God's Ambassadors: A History of the Christian Clergy in America*. Grand Rapids, Mich.: Eerdmans, 2007.

———. *A History of Pastoral Care in America: From Salvation to Self-Realization*. Nashville: Abingdon, 1983.

Keller, Rosemary Skinner, Gerald F. Moede, and Mary Elizabeth Moore, eds. *Called to Serve: The United Methodist Diaconate*. Nashville: United Methodist General Board of Higher Education and Ministry, 1987.

Kirby, James E., Russell E. Richey, and Kenneth E. Rowe. *The Methodists.* Westport, Conn.: Greenwood, 1996.

Maryniak, Benedict R., and John Wesley Brinsfield, Jr. *The Spirit Divided: Memoirs of Civil War Chaplains: The Union.* Macon, Ga.: Mercer University Press, 2007.

Matthaei, Sondra Higgins. *The United Methodist Deacon: Servant Ministry in the Communion of the Trinity* (Monograph). Nashville: General Board of Higher Education and Ministry, The United Methodist Church, 2003.

Matthews, Rex D. *Timetables of History for Students of Methodism.* Nashville: Abingdon, 2007.

McClain, William B. *Black People in the Methodist Church.* Cambridge: Schenkman Publishing, 1984.

Messer, Donald E., ed., *Send Me? The Itineracy in Crisis.* Nashville: Abingdon, 1991.

Neville, Robert Cummings. *A Theological Analysis of the Order of Deacons in The United Methodist Church* (Monograph). Nashville: General Board of Higher Education and Ministry, The United Methodist Church, 2002.

Quarterly Review: A Journal of Theological Resources for Ministry. Nashville: General Board of Higher Education and Ministry, The United Methodist Church, and The United Methodist Publishing House, 1980–2005. Complete archive available free of charge online at http://www.quarterlyreview.org.

Richey, Russell E. *Early American Methodism.* Bloomington and Indianapolis: Indiana University Press, 1991.

———. *The Methodist Conference in America.* Nashville: Kingswood, 1996.

Richey, Russell E., Dennis M. Campbell, and William B. Lawrence, eds. *Connectionalism: Ecclesiology, Mission, and Identity.* United Methodist and American Culture Series. Volume 1. Nashville: Abingdon, 1997.

———. *Doctrines and Discipline: Methodist Theology and Practice.* United Methodist and American Culture Series. Volume 3. Nashville: Abingdon, 1999.

———. *Marks of Methodism: Practices of Ecclesiology.* United Methodism and American Culture Series. Volume 5. Nashville: Abingdon, 2005.

————. *The People(s) Called Methodist: Forms and Reforms of Their Life.* United Methodism and American Culture Series. Volume 2. Nashville: Abingdon, 1998.

————. *Questions for the Twenty-First Century Church.* United Methodism and American Culture Series. Volume 4. Nashville: Abingdon, 1999.

Richey, Russell E., Kenneth E. Rowe, Jean Miller Schmidt, *The Methodist Experience in America.* Nashville: Abingdon, 2000.

Robert, Dana L. *American Women in Mission: A Social History of Their Thought and Practice.* Macon, Ga.: Mercer University Press, 1996.

Shockley, Grant S., ed. *Heritage and Hope: The African-American Presence in United Methodism.* Nashville: Abingdon, 1991.

Tewksbury, Donald G. *The Founding of American Colleges and Universities Before the Civil War.* New York: Arno Press and The New York Times, 1969.

Tigert, Jno. J. *A Constitutional History of American Episcopal Methodism*, 3rd ed., rev. and enl. Nashville: Publishing House of the Methodist Episcopal Church, South, 1908.

Thomas, James S. *Methodism's Racial Dilemma: The Story of the Central Jurisdiction.* Nashville: Abingdon, 1992.